A Series of Underscores

By: Jon Koegle

"A Series of Underscores"

By: Jon Koegle

July 14th of 2015

Published through www.createspace.com

ISBN-13: 978-1515075301

ISBN-10: 1515075303

Contents

Introduction

The Mind Unseen

Where do I begin? Where do I start? Well, we all have to start somewhere otherwise you wouldn't be here. Speaking of starting, this is actually the first book I've ever written. I wanted to produce something different than your average book on the shelf. However, now you don't even need a shelf to put books on. My, have times changed. Today, there are many digital books out there. Regardless of paper or from a computer image, these books all start or form in the mind. As you read, this book will enter your mind. So in a way it's like I'm actually entering into many minds, just not having access to everything. I do, however, have an opportunity to help produce change. Change the way we live, how we think and what we do. So as these words enter your mind, in a way you're receiving a piece of my mind. I say only a piece, because the mind is capable of so much – yet we tend to use only so little. I want to encourage the readers to really stand out and make a difference.

I'm making it my personal duty to give a few copies of this book away. I urge you, if you have received this book for free at no charge; please make it your personal duty to give this away as well. After you are done reading it, give it away so it can continue to touch lives. You may want to give it to a complete stranger or someone you hardly know. Be a part of a cycle that wants to see others become successful more than ourselves. Be a part of passing down opportunity for change among people that live in the atmosphere around you. It's time we stepped outside of our comfort zones, facing reality as we become successful as a team, as a unit. It's time we laid down our pride, truly asking for help knowing we can't do it alone. A lot more can be accomplished as pride fades and humility rises. Have an open heart to allow truth to come in and change the hearts, developing compassion for others. Be willing to lend helping hands for those who struggle in life, because we all do at some point in time.

At times, I believe many choose not to truly state what is on their minds. I know our body language can stand out when things are not going as planned. We become grumpy or move at a very fast pace. Others become depressed or quiet when they are normally very talkative. Some even play it off very well, just putting on shows and deceiving many. However, even though the show goes on, deep down inside the curtain calls. We are not a question without an answer. We are all called for greatness, in which our identity awakens more as we reach out to the lost. We are so much more than worthless and I can assure you that we all have a purpose. Be encouraged to speak your mind to let others know what you're going through. It's better to open up to others than to stay silent and lie to ourselves. I believe as others see a new positive perspective in your life, this will give them a hope for something new. This will give them a hope for something fresh and fruitful. Often, it's not the rocky climb that stops us from traveling over a mountain… No, most of the time, it's a small pebble irritating us in a way where we will choose not to advance. To advance forward, we must choose to deal with our issues in a positive manner. Many choose not to deal with the small issues that go on in our lives and would rather cope with them by doing things that either harms us or others.

It's time we faced reality, focusing on the solutions and not the problems. It's time our minds were seen, regardless if others don't like the ideas produced. Brainstorm; make ideas brighter, bigger, and better. Don't be afraid to take risks. Control your mind to produce a positive change and become somebody that cares. Our eyes become useless when our mind is blind. If we are not willing to produce some type of change or transformation, then we will be stuck as our same old selves. Nothing new would be evident in our lives. Have an open mind when you read this book and don't be afraid to design or create new ideas to place into action. I don't believe a positive life can come from a mind that is negative all the time. Do you mind? If not, then you're ready to begin the first chapter, which is chapter 07. Don't mind the order in which the chapters are given. I wanted to produce something different; training my "mind" to be open, because a closed one is dangerous.

Even though I'm not there in person, I would like to thank you for choosing to read this book. It was out of your own free will that you chose to do this. I don't believe anyone forced you to read this, but if so hopefully something struck your mind besides the item another held against you. Anyways, I'd like to talk about free will for just one bit while we are on the subject. Here are a few bible scriptures that go along to tie in what is said.

2nd Peter 3:9 states, "The Lord is not slow in keeping his promise, as some understand slowness. Instead he is patient with you, not wanting anyone to perish, but everyone to come to repentance.

Romans 12:16-18 states, "Live in harmony with one another. Do not be proud, but be willing to associate with people of low position. Do not be conceited. Do not repay anyone evil for evil. Be careful to do what is right in the eyes of everyone. If it is possible, as far as it depends on you, live at peace with everyone.

Proverbs 18:20-21 states, "From the fruit of their mouth a person's stomach is filled; with the harvest of their lips they are satisfied. The tongue has the power of life and death, and those who love it will eat its fruit.

2nd Timothy 1:7 states, "For the Spirit God gave us does not make us timid, but gives us power, love and self-discipline.

I'd like to encourage all the readers to strive for positivity. Choose to look at the bright side of all situations and speak life into the darkness. What we choose to believe really does make an impact in either a positive or negative way, so why not choose positive? As you continue to read these chapters, be open to receive and believe. I believe as this book reaches out to others, change will come to those who are willing to produce something new and effective.

The beauty of free will is that God is patient, willing to wait for us to choose Him. God does not demand us to come to Him for this would not be out of Love. Any authority figure in our lives should be a role model, which we can learn and grow to become stronger and more effective. If this authority figure abuses his authority out of hate, then most likely we will not have any acknowledgment or respect for this person. Regardless of others actions, we are to submit to our authority as long as it's not sinful. However, if we are driven by fear since we think there will be punishment if we don't do as directed, then most likely when they are not in or around our lives anymore we will just go back doing the same old things and no growth will come from the situations we have experienced.

Only out of love comes true change and transformation. Leaders who are patient with their employees are willing to serve and express their concern while even helping them to produce positive results. Leaders that truly express love should come along side to help them succeed. It's always good to talk about how to grow to do the jobs better, but those who chose to include some type of way to bring forth different perspectives or analogies tend to reach others more efficiently. They relate to other scenarios that happened to express different viewpoints, which are far more effective and powerful. Furthermore, when we take time to actually have a one on one conversation with one another, true friendship and relationships are either restored or formed further. For when others actually feel accepted and loved, then the right choice is usually easier to make. When we are forceful by demanding and expecting things from others, walls are built tending to shut down a relationship regardless if it was strong or hardly into existence.

Our actions should affect others by producing positive results.

Another person's actions, if negative, should not affect our walk in regards to growing closer with God. At this moment, we pretty much have three choices. We can correct the person, join in conversation and stirring up negativity, or walk away. As we are firmly planted upon His Solid Foundation, we should not easily stray to the left or to the right. I truly believe that God actually uses situations to draw us closer to Him.

If we choose to correct a person, we should first make sure that we are at peace. I've learned it's best to yield myself to God's calling and allow His words to be spoken through us as directed by His Holy Spirit. The words that come out should be out of love for God does not condemn. Also, we are not to bring forth any conviction, for the Holy Spirit will do that. The Love that is expressed should be evident, which will change the atmosphere around where God is dwelling. We must yield and recognize that it is God doing it through us. Those who listen can either accept what is being said or have no part of it. If they choose to not accept the Love expressed, then simply end the conversation in a loving manner. If we continue, tension may rise which then nothing gets accomplished and things get haywire. As we learn to yield and allow God to use us, the truth is expressed and a seeds are planted.

If we choose to join in conversation with the negativity, then we become vulnerable and are just as guilty. We will be affected by the situation because we have allowed it. It's like we automatically have given into defeat. Those planted firm upon God's word should be full of courage and power, willing to express Love. I know joining in these types of conversations, not only affect us, it affects the relationship that we have with God as well. We must learn to use what God has implanted and strive for righteousness.

If we choose to simply just walk away, our walk should not be affected, yet no love or reason is expressed. It's ok if we choose to walk away so we can gain peace and understanding to correctly handle situations for the future. We choose to walk away not to show that we are weak, yet so that our walk with God does not decay. If possible, it might be best to at least go back to the person and express out of love why we chose to walk away. I would recommend doing this when the time is right as we are illuminated with God's presence and peace, especially yielding ourselves to what He wants to say through us. I know by staying calm and collective, while having a soft voice can be more reachable than choosing to have a harsh loud tone.

Another person's actions, if positive, will usually affect our walk in a positive manner. Positive actions are usually helpful, producing enthusiasm, as well as motivation towards others. Seeds are planted and seen even in and through action. I can understand if others don't want to "hear" about positive things and want nothing to do with the Gospel or our changed lives... However, if it is only through action, then no words are expressed – UNLESS – they ask, "Why are we so different?" They might ask this because it should be noticeable. Then we have an opportunity to express the loving testimony that illuminated us. God's presence is beaming not only in us but around us as well.

I know that when I was living a life of destruction, I chose to be negative. Others actions affected me negatively because I was already negative. Others around me that were negative did cause my actions to dig even further into negativity. However, this was still by choice, for we are all lead astray by our own sinful desires. When I was already led astray, pursing my own sinful desire, more fuel was poured on that fire because of the people I chose to hang out and associate myself with. However, I can tell you and know in my heart that the positive people around me at this time never forced me to change. It was always by choice. I'll never forget the Love that was expressed along with even later, hearing about the prayers that were said and answered. This was far more effective than force. They were patient, choosing not to give up on me, expressing love, and never backing down from placing their faith in God. Fruitful change came and is now evident in my life as well as many prayers answered. My mind is now open to truth and no longer closed, feeding on the lies that once made my identity. All Glory to God!

CHAPTER 07

Thinking… Thinking… Thinking…

Life… so what's it all about? Is it more than just a bunch of random words put together to make sentences that sometimes plain don't make since? It has to be more than just typing a bunch of random letters, because once I do that… gflaie comes out from it and does it make sense? However, it may be possible that gflaie just might happen to make since to someone out there. Let's just say that gflaie means bookstore. Did you pick this up in a bookstore, testing the first page to even seem like it might be interesting? Did you buy this because of the front cover? Or perhaps you're reading it because the front cover looks attracting or interesting? At times we do the same to people. We judge others by their appearance or even the fact that they might use spell check to help them spell the word properly. A business man comes into a store with a suit and tie, usually treated with respect. Across town, a hard working man covered in dirt and sweat, being judged by what he wears, possibly is given dirty looks. Why do we treat others differently based on what they wear, how they talk, the way their body language comes into play? What if I told you that this same business man has a heart of stone, just putting on a show to get what he wants and to make others feel good? Deep down inside that nice suit is a sawed off shot gun just waiting to explode! What if the people interacting with him are putting on a show as well, just because it's their job and that's what customers expect? Or possibly they even want something from the man? Or even possibly themselves want to be or feel accepted? What if I told you the hard working man has a heart of gold that is fine and pure, yet when he engages in a conversation there is a lack of attention and others choose not to engage, either switching the subject or completely ignoring him. Deep down inside he has a passion to reach out to others, yet others push him away. How is your heart? Are you sensitive to others needs? And, what we have, is it truly our property? Do we put on shows to impress others? Are we really being REAL and enjoying life? Adjotieqjkng I felt like typing that just to be real in this book. At times I don't know what to type or what words sound best to fit inside of a sentence to make since. This might not even make since to some, yet to others it does. In your own personal life – is it all about you or are you actually interested in seeing others succeed beyond yourself? I got to go now, yet I'll be back typing some random statements from the mind of Jon Koegle.

I'm back... not actually. I'm Jon Koegle. To me there is no such thing as "normal". What would that even look like? We all have different opinions and statements. We all do not think alike. We have different ideas or even different ways to do things. We were not called to be professionals, yet it seems sometimes the harder we try the more and more we dig ourselves to nowhere, in which I'm now here. Then we sometimes beat ourselves up and feel sorry for ourselves. Know that we are already considered perfect as for who we are. There is something bright and brilliant to be discovered beyond the darkness that surpasses us. I mean we all didn't start out that way. We chose to develop a lifestyle that we live today. There is no such thing as a bad kid... just a kid that chooses to do bad things. Doesn't anyone have any common sense today, you might ask? In the first paragraph, you may have realized that the word since was misspelled or misused since, since was supposed to be sense. Make since? However you would like to say it, put it, or possibly think it. You could relate this to me – do I have any common sense? This author doesn't know even how to spell or use words correctly. That's Odd? What if I told you I used the word since wrongly on purpose just to get your senses moving? Make sense? And what's so "common" about that? I've gained cents. Especially if you're buying my book because of that statement. Are you alert? Focused? Do I have your attention? And out of all the money we make here on earth, where does it go? What do we buy or invest? Some would call me a loser if I chose to invest it to help change and develop lives. Seeing changed lives is the best investment anyone could make. Is it possible to fit a mansion and an expensive car inside a coffin? I suppose if it were a giants coffin, or even if it were the items from some small people off of Gulliver's Travels. Let's face it... This is reality, not a make believe fairytale. Do fairies even have tails? The imagination has no end or limit unless you put one on it. The sky is not the limit here or ever... Continue to dream and be an inspiration toward others, because all and all we as people are the only thing that goes after we die.

By now if you're still reading, you're hopefully sucked in like a tractor beam or locked on like a heat seeking missile. You might be wondering why I started with Chapter 7? Don't worry this book won't self destruct by the time you get to Chapter 1 and I have no intention of informing you how to build a missile or in that fact setting one off. Unless, however, it's in your mind. It just takes a little push of a button anyway. Are you tired of others consistently pushing your buttons? I mean, we paid for that remote, so why do we choose to let others press our buttons? Nothing should rob us from having peace. At times while growing up we believe lies about ourselves... how we think we are not good enough or won't amount to anything. I graduated high school at the year 00', in which our class called us the "Class of Nothing". Don't believe the lies and make something out of nothing. We all are called for greatness! Why start off with Chapter 1 anyway. Doesn't that get boring? Oh, look a new book... yup, chapter 1 again. Does anyone even notice? Or is it just an all actual knowing "common" thing to do? Doesn't anyone else want something different and unique? It's amazing to live in this day and age with all the technology. Broken pencils are pretty much pointless, pens eventually run out of ink... I just hope there isn't a power surge as I type this. OOPS, THE CAPS LOCK CAME ON. That's better. Let's see where was I? Oh, ya... Some might possibly use the Lord's name in vain when their buttons are pushed. They might even have some awkward things to say about this book. I wonder to those if they ever tried using their own name instead or even just some random phrase? Ahh Fiddle Sticks! I mean can you really play the fiddle with a stick? I suppose you could. Quite possibly this phrase is a bar and grill, in which that case I'm sure you would see or hear #!@%... This could mean more than a blot to block out cussing. To some they see symbols, to others possibly a form of art. Go ahead and Google it, Fiddle Sticks; a pub in New York... while #!@%; nothing. Some might say Google knows everything. I hope you don't believe that lie. Truth: There truly is a living God that knows everything, is patient, and loves us more than we know, however the day or hour is unknown, we must be prepared, we reap what we sow.

So we reap what we sow; so in order to reap we must sow something. What are we sowing out there? I know if we sew garments then we have clothing that was repaired, making it last a little longer than before. If farmers sow seeds, then they reap an abundant harvest. However, to make it abundant, it does take a lot of commitment, dedication, and devotion. I mean let's face it... They can't just go out to a field and plant a few seeds, do nothing, wait about 3 months and expect the best of the best. It would be pretty hilarious to see however. A farmer yelling at his crop because of how terrible it came out and why it can't just grow properly or stronger. Yet in our everyday lives, people do just that. Do we really go above and beyond protocol at our jobs? Are we doing this for our boss, only to get recognized in for a possible promotion? Are we actually working placing our heart and effort for the better of the company? It's best to do this for our Creator, not expecting anything in return. Setting goals and achieving them throughout the year are very important keys in life. Which keys you might ask? Well actually you have 2 keys to choose from if you're referring to computer keys. I, F – which spells "if" since they are very important keys "in" life. If I do this and if I do that. If I tore some pages out of this book would you still purchase it? Could of, should of, would of… Make Moves or Make Excuses! The point is it's just vital. I wouldn't be surprised if and when the boss is not around – if not more than half of the company loses heart and doesn't work as efficient. Honestly, we need to care and make a stand. We should work just as hard, if not harder when our boss is not around. And so what if he comes back and does not notice how much was achieved. Do you actually need confirmation? Does it make you feel all warm and gooey inside? Wait, that might be a chocolate chip cookie or a hot fudge brownie that you're craving for right now. It's ok to place this book down and go get it, if it's within reason. It's great hearing from a living God, knowing your doing your best especially when it's for Him. It does feel good to hear uplifting statements from our co-workers. By all means, regardless if anyone hasn't said anything encouraging to you… say something encouraging to them. Do your co-workers lack enthusiasm? Be an encouragement and get this party started! Why would you even want to work at job you hate to do? Yet many people do it today. This doesn't need to be. Regardless of the job where people are at, there has to be some way to encourage others and make them feel good about themselves and where they are at. I challenge you to find something good to say that is encouraging to everyone in your work area. You might just be surprised about the comments that you'll receive from the feedback or possibly the reactions you'll get.

Let's face it; words… they can either lift us up or tear us down. I have no idea who will read this book, but if I wrote this book in regards to how stupid, fat and retarded the readers are, you most likely would place this book down instantly. Hopefully you have not.

I have a feeling some, yet hopefully only few actually did just that. However, I, myself, would be calling me the same due to the simple fact that I'm reading this as I type. You might even try to find out where I live, breaking my door down, and unleash a fury of vengeance. This was not my intention at all, by no means, to strike a match and ignite a fire. Yet if you are offended where did that feeling come from? I have learned that the lies stored up inside of us produce negative feelings. So, in order to receive truth from them, we need to trust in God – allowing him to speak truth into our past. After all, He is the only one that can. It's not like there is a time machine built allowing us to travel back to make different choices to better the outcome in life. Beam me up Scotty! Wait, that's Star Trek... Back to the Future would have been the proper choice, however at this moment; I'm not sure what phrase to say from the movie... Manure, I hate manure! Ah, Yes... That's it. So, if you're willing, ask God anytime why you feel hurt and ask Him to show you where this feeling came from. Once he does, some might be astonished. Let God know how you feel in the memory or possibly memories that He shows you. Wait for His TRUTH to come and receive it. Receive it by speaking out loud what God says through your conscience. That is having faith and believing in an all powerful God that loves us more than we know. The sheep hear His voice. He is the true Shepherd, follow Him. Continue to build your relationship up with Him. Communicate and let Him know what you are going through, even allow him to be a part of our every day busy lives. -

Let's rewind words for just a tad.bɒt ɒ tƨuႱ ɿoʇ ƨbɿow bniwɘɿ ƨ'tɘ⅃ -

If I wrote this book in regards to how smart, intelligent, and productive the readers are, you might actually continue to read, which you are if you are. Reading... Reading... Reading... Some might not think of themselves as smart or intelligent. Some might wonder why they even exist, just wanting a fast exit out. I, myself, don't find that true. Regardless of who you are reading my book, I believe somewhere deep down there is something special about you. Possibly a gift that hasn't been discovered and just waiting, wanting to explode as it comes out. Filling yourself or possibly others with more inspiration, ideas, and wonder. We are all made differently, yet equal through the eyes of God. I want to encourage those to never give up, never stop trying, and to say YES to life. Continue to enhance and amplify your gifts and talents in life. Regardless if others do not like your ideas, continue to experiment and let your imagination fly! Continue to put up the good fight. Try new things, regardless if it takes time to learn. This might feel uncomfortable at first and it's is ok to feel that. When we step outside of ourselves in what we are so used to all the time, uncomfortable happens. Yet this doesn't mean you can't find peace in doing that. Don't let or allow others to tear you down. Find true joy, because happiness only lasts a short while.

Are you happy or joyful? I admit trying to fill ourselves up with material things only produces happiness for a short while. We have the mindsets in a today's age and generation where we want the latest thing that is out there. We not only want what's out there, we want it NOW. Most are not willing to wait for it and have some type of patience. We live in a microwave generation, coming out like pop corn... pop, pop, pop. Cold Pop, Cold Pop, Barbecuing, Barbecuing... (very few will understand this) Doesn't anyone like surprises anymore? Most want to know what they even got for Christmas before the time even comes... You remember sneaking into your parent's room, finding the presents, unwrapping a tiny corner and taping it back shut so they won't notice. Then when the time comes we act like we are all excited when we open it putting on a show. We let our fake smiles and enthusiasm motions hit the fan and scatter across the room. I wonder if we would have still received the presents if our parents found out. Whether or not the weather permits it does not make since. People will drive in a storm to acquire something they absolutely want. Yet at times, we don't do the same for things that we might need. It's better to have and not need than to need and not have . So what are we stocking up so we have, yet don't need? An abundance of clothes, shoes, video games, movies, cologne, all the makeup... here let me draw you a line. __________________ Feel free to fill in this blank while you're at it. Maybe you need more than one blank. Here, here's another line or should I say a series of underscores? ____________________. It just might possibly be that, that line was not long enough? ____. There, hope that helps. If you are reading this digitally I hope you don't actually write on the screen. Anyway, does all this stuff really make us happy? Most of you can agree, we continue to want more and more, yet we still feel empty inside. It's like building a castle in the sand. All that weight with no foundation and what we have built up will not last. Unless, however, it's a castle out of sand. Remember playing in the sand at a beach or a sand pit, building and constructing things? Perhaps you had Lego's or Lincoln Logs instead? Filling ourselves up with material things does not fill that emptiness. Joy however does. When you fulfill something that you have a passion for, I believe Joy is produced. When you achieve a goal that will have an impact on yourself as well as others. When we see others have a more successful day, just because we enlightened them with a few words and some compliments came out from it. When we see others mourning turn into a smile because of the comfort that was needed. Be encouraged to place others and their needs before our own and see what comes out from it. Regardless of what time of day, dream.

Did you actually take some time to pause from reading to think back over your life? Did you take a break just to "day dream" for a bit? I did while writing this. Writing this book takes quite a bit of time, more than I expected. However, I know it's not time wasted. Time, a precious thing to waste. We only have a total of twenty four hours in a day to accomplish tasks, dreams, visions, or whatever we need or possibly want to accomplish. At times, we just want to have fun. There is nothing wrong with having fun; however are the more important tasks done first in the day? As when we choose to have fun, we can get caught up in it loosing track of time. I believe it's wise to choose to work before play. Yet, it is a choice, in which I can't force you to do. This book can't force you to do it either. Wouldn't that would be a site to see... a book forcing someone to do something? I'm sure it's already happened in a cartoon. Anyways, back to reality... At times we choose to occupy ourselves with little effort, participating in what we, ourselves would rather do than what's more important. Time is something we do not get back. What's done is done, and what's done is in the past. Even as you read this "what's done" is behind you now as you continue to read. To some, I wouldn't be surprised if some comments came out probably saying that this book is a waste of time. Maybe it is to you at this moment. Maybe you have something more important to do. You know, you could always place some type of book mark right here. Just in case you don't have one __________ there, maybe you'll mark it. Maybe becomes either a Yes or a No as you choose the outcome of actually marking it. Maybe you might have a son or a daughter wanting to spend more time together. Possibly a mother or a father or any family. Family, to me, does not necessarily need to be in tree line either. Be encouraged to spend some more time with family and friends that mean a lot in your life. Be there for them, encourage them to succeed and help them be successful. Would you like to write down the time? ___________ Even though at times, regardless of what time of day, it's beginning to become that time of night.

Depending on when you're reading this, good morning, evening, or night. Good Night! Tired? I was wondering why the keys were getting biggerrrrrrr........galllllllllllllllllllerpi – then it hit me. However it would be weird if the laptop actually hit me. I should rephrase it and say I hit the laptop, pretty much counting ZzzZzzz's.

Why is it usually Zzz's or sheep as others say? Do they think of themselves as Shepherd's attending a flock? Don't they realize so many sheep are being led astray, wondering about as they please? Is it even possible for sheep to hop over a fence? Shepherds truly lay down their lives for the sheep. If one is led astray or gone about missing, would you go about to find it or would you stay with the rest of the pack, not caring about the lost ones? Once found, would you rejoice and celebrate afterwards? So many of us don't care about those who are lost and lead astray. We sometimes label them as outcast or so much more. Regardless, I challenge you to be in the world not of the world... Placing labels on others: "Hello, My Name Is ______" Or do we choose to take it beyond that? You might wonder why I entitled this book, "A Series of Underscores". Call it what you will, call it what you want. This book is nameless with no label, until you choose what to call it. Wait? You might ask, "Doesn't this book already have a title?" In very fine print, yes. However, I would like you to decide as well. Go ahead; feel free to write on the line given because a series of underscores produces a blank line. Some might say a flat line. However I can assure you even though this book has no heart beat, it is alive; full of rhythm, thoughts, ideas, etc... We go about our busy lives doing things that we want to do. It's all about me, It's all about I. Why? I, I, I, My, My, My.... Well, I would like to see people start to care for one another out there. Children lost, People with no shelter, the sick that need healed. There is so much. When is the last time we have actually helped a stranger? Someone that we don't possibly even know. If we have the mindset of thinking they will use the blessing for inappropriate use, then why not sit down with them and pay for their meal or even purchase what they need? Get to know them and develop a relationship. And even doing so, do we have the mindset of expecting something back in return? If not from the stranger, then from someone else? I have heard some stories of those who choose to help others, then getting blessed back in return. I would have to say, most of the time the blessing that comes back is unexpected. Just to reach out to others from the kindness of our hearts is passionate. It's really cool to pass down these good deeds from and to others, allowing the people we help to also make a choice, in choosing to bless other strangers as well. So whatever you choose to call my book, would it be because you wanted to call it that? Or would it be because someone else inspired you to call it that? Regardless, I know this will bring some brain storming waves your way.

Chapter 06

Windows Become Doors

Do any of you recall sneaking out at night while living with your parents? You might have gone through a window perhaps? I'm hoping that the window was open before you actually went through it. And what was so important to do at that time of hour? Go to a party? Hang out with friends? Perhaps a girlfriend? Regardless, it's a choice that was chosen, in which you had to live with the consequences. This could go two ways; either the consequences of getting caught by our parents, or the cost of something bad happening. For me, personally, I can relate to both. Sneaking out, even stealing the car to go on a joy ride, and then getting into trouble where someone bashed in our side finder. We all can relate to something similar throughout our lives. Wanting to have our way of so called "fun", then out of the red something unexpected happens. Why does it always have to be "out of the blue"? For this book, I'm choosing a different color. Why not say out of the red instead? Well, as you can tell I just did. Anyways, on top of that, the next day coming up with a story; lying to our mother how a basketball hit the car leaving the side finder all bashed in. Really? A basketball did that much damage? WOW!? It must have been traveling at the speed of light! And for that fact, not once, but numerous times! I remember paying for that choice, a nice shinny penny I might add... then adding up to like ten thousand pennies more. Remember that brother? I'm sure you do, Craig was with us. That window became a door to consequences we had to endure. So what "windows" are we leaving open that could damage our future, to where we have to pay a price?

There are many choices in life that we choose on a daily basis, just don't let those choices choose you. Wouldn't that be odd? Choices choosing us? Let's face it, we choose what we do in our everyday busy lives. We decide what we do throughout the day and how the time is spent. Like buying a watch, now that's time spent. And what do we choose to watch? There is so much garbage on T.V. in today's day and age. Is it even worth the time spent? Sure it can be entertaining, but what are we focusing on that we allow to enter our mind? Windows that open penetrate the mind, if not shut eventually become wide open doors. What windows are we leaving open? I, myself, am leaving Microsoft Windows open as I type this. I am using Windows 7 by the way just in case you are wondering. However, since I don't see seven windows anywhere in relation to that, I'll just give you seven. If I choose to leave a window open that floods my mind with garbage, wouldn't I eventually become trash? And who would want that? I'm so thankful for a Living God that actually loves us for who we are. He saw through the filth that I once built up and gave me a new life. The mind is a powerful thing to waist and must say not even compared to waste. You might say, look at this author wasting his time again. He misused another word. Well, if so it's a choice you'll have to make. Like I stated in Chapter 7, well – you get the picture. Don't let your mind go to waste. I challenge you to continue to dream and be an inspiration to others out there, using your creative imagination – full of thoughts and ideas. Use them to help reach others out there in a world that's dying. Let's bring back the life!

So, let's see what's on T.V. shall we? Now, where did I place that remote? It amazes me that we will search for minutes upon minutes trying to find a remote, instead of actually pushing the button on the actual television set. Ah, here it is, found it between the cushions along with a nice tuna on rye sandwich! Mmmm. Anyways, back to what's on the tube... *CLICK* Nope, BORING...

Next! *CLICK*, *CLICK*, *CLI-* HOLD UP... Yup, a nice fine waist and so much more. A woman showing off her cleavage and God knows what else. Many times we choose to stop at channels that draw attention to our eyes. We then take it a step further, wondering what our lives might be like if we were with that significant other. Sometimes, we still take it a step further, going beyond that and so much more. By the time you're done reading this my clothes might be out of style. As if we are thinking about clothes in the first place? If we choose to leave this window open, it eventually turns into lust. We must choose to make a covenant with our eyes and instead of stopping at those certain channels, develop a positive habit into skipping those channels. Perhaps even do some research before watching a movie or yet why not fast forward the scene. If I choose to fast forward thorugh this book my tyipng becomes all messed ups nad this is what coems out. Even though the words were misspelled you were still able to read them. Same thing happens when we choose to fast forward a scene, in our mind we still know what's going on. It doesn't take that much of an imagination to figure that out. However, if I choose to skip a scene, at least it's over and done with not drawing attention to my eyes and penetrating the mind. Let's see what's on another channel, shall we? Like you have a choice... Well, yah, you actually do if you choose to stop reading. By the way, this tuna on rye is delicious! Anyways, where did I put that remote? Oh, yah... *CLICK*

"The President!" Well, nothing to talk about on that channel... *CLICK*

Ah... here we go, a perfect scenario. Some mid aged people getting all excited by strolling into a walk in fridge full of beer, later in a limo arriving at a hot spot, or even doing something ridiculous like jumping out of a plane with no parachute all for some beer... Advertisements about alcohol usually focus on having a so called "fun" time... Hmmm, interesting. They only choose to inform those watching part of the picture, in which the entire picture becomes *out of place*. Please, don't adjust your eyes I'll help you put out of place back in place. The ads leave out scenes from the final results. I don't remember watching any of these commercials with people getting drunk that result in passing out at a party or even getting arrested. I believe these types of commercials put a spin on the truth. Not once do I recall waking up with a hangover in jail ever becoming a "fun" time. Not to mention having a friend, "Ralph". You know "Ralph", throwing up, possibly waking up in his own vomit. Yup, I mentioned it. Yet many do, and choose to go back to it. I know this might sound disgusting, yet it's the truth. I hope you didn't "Ralph" on this page... you might want to buy another copy. Many are lead astray, possibly thinking, I'll only have a few drinks." Yet two turn into four and four turn into floor. If not the floor, then possibly stumbling into walls, swerving to hit parked cars. "I can quit anytime", some might say. "I don't have a problem, I can control it." Then why do we choose to want more, going back to what made us sick in the first place? Are you sure you can control it or is the "so called fun" controlling you? Many choose to deny the truth and choose to live in darkness. The darkness consumes us, leaving us blind and vulnerable to the lies. We believe we'll have a good time, possibly meet the right person of our dreams. Possibly get noticed and finally be the popular type. We believe that things will get better, yet we drown our problems instead of facing them. The problems are still there, yet we find ways to "cope" with our issues. Well, I've personally had it with this lifestyle, let's change the channel. *CLICK*

Ah... One of many favorite shows out there "COPS". I highly find it ironic that those who hate cops still choose to watch the show "COPS". Yet this is a different subject. Anyway, back to the show! Yes!!! A high speed pursuit! Well, at least I thought it might be...

Swerve, miss, Swerve, miss... pretty boring. Finally! The chase comes to a halt. Come to find out this wasn't a chase at all. The officer realizes that there might be some regards to drinking and driving. Any readers here remember getting pulled over and ran a number of tests? *Like I can actually take a count* Do you recall placing your left foot in front of your right foot, or was it your right foot in front of your left? And No, I'm not relating to the hokey pokey dance either... *TRIP... STuMbLe* Regardless, I'm talking about walking a series of underscores... If you haven't figured that phrase out yet and are wondering what I mean, I could draw it out for you. _______ There, I just did. However, I didn't draw it, just typed it. So, back to the show. The officer has the driver out of the car realizing he can't walk a straight line. Now, he is ready to do a sobriety test. Do you recall any sobriety tests? One usually blows into the machine so that it does a measure of one's alcohol level in that individual's breath. Instead of blowing, the poor old soul ends up drinking from the breathalyzer. This might sound and look funny; however inside he is hurt and dying. Off he goes to jail due to leaving a dirty window open that eventually became a wide open door. At least he is in jail now. I'm just happy he didn't wreck or hit another person, possibly taking a life. What if that was your life? Or possibly a friends or family members? You could ask, will a licensed to kill, steal a life? Wouldn't you rather save a life? Many still choose to leave those windows wide open, eventually shattering the glass. If not from a wreck, then from wrecking their lives as well as others... I feel your pain because I've been there and done that. I can assure you it's no fun at all. I hope you don't choose to make the same mistakes. It's up to us to actually listen to advise and apply it in and through our actions.

Speaking of action, let's see what's on the news. Lights, Camera, Action! *CLICK* It seems as if there is hardly anything positive on the news anymore. 7 dead in a killing, racists jokes, all about the celebrities, others throwing parties, what to wear, what not to wear… like it matters anyway if it's coming off? Right? Wrong! It actually does matter. Where are we working at? Let's face it, if we were working at a bank I'm pretty sure we would get fired coming in wearing a greasy stained up white tee and a pair of torn ripped up shorts. Even though this person might have a great heart, his outfit is not suitable for the position he is placed in. I know, it's the heart that matters, yet first impressions can give others some dirty looks. Do we have the mindset to dress in modesty? Do we care what our children wear? Do you actually think a mechanic would come into a shop to work on a vehicle dressed in an expensive suit? Alrighty Then!!! Let's get down to business! YEAH! Do we choose to wear clothing just to attract attention? If so, why? There has to be a reason behind that. Possibly a lie believed, neglecting the truth. Do we wear certain clothing just so we can "be noticed"? Maybe we choose to wear outfits just because it's today's "style" and we just want to fit in. Are you tired of actually fitting in and still feeling empty on the inside? Be who you are and how you were created and designed to be. Don't become someone else. I'm writing this book just to be different, choosing not to fit in with the rest of the world. I have a tendency on placing something out there that has never been done before. Maybe you have some ideas of your own? Are you afraid of what others might think or say? Why? Choose to take a risk and give it a shot! Anyways, let's get back to the news!

Oh, exciting!!! This just in! Brace yourself! Breaking News!!! A new book entitled, "A Series of Underscores" is climbing, working its way to the top of the charts! Wow! Incredible!!! It's not even a well known author either… Who the heck is Jon Koegle? Let's hear what others have to say about it. Others love it already, saying that the book is thought provoking, something different compared to what has already been placed out on the shelf, and it captures the attention of those who choose to read it. Some might even say it's the book that never collects dust! How Astonishing!!! Ok, so maybe

I'm over exaggerating. Even though this statement is not yet true, one thing that comes to mind that is actual TRUTH is those smoking commercials. And by smoking well, you know what I'm talking about? They start out on how "cool" it might seem to smoke with people dancing, making music, and doing all sorts of stuff. Then towards the end you see a cancer victim from smoking sitting in a wheel chair out on his last breath. He chooses to use his last words to try and touch the lives of those either still in the process of doing it or at least give out some type of warning to those who are not doing it. Some advice, either to stay away from smoking or at least warning them, yes, this is what it does... Look at me and see what it has done to me. I recall even watching a commercial with a guy having to use some type of voice amplifier because his vocal cord is decomposing eventually coming to a point of actually being destroyed. Yet people still choose to smoke and choose not care about these warnings that could possibly come crashing down on their lives. This goes far beyond smoking and drinking as well. What about all the harmful substances out there? What about eating fast food all the time? Don't you want to live a healthy productive life? It's up to us to choose. We only have one body, in which it's the temple to the Holy Spirit. Don't you know if we choose to intake all these harmful things it affects God's Spirit? Well, if you didn't, you know now. Tired of the News? Or are you tired of hearing the truth in the news? Let's take a quick commercial break... I'll be back after a few messages. *CLICK*

Joe Boxer: You remember kids picking on one another in school. You might be possibly walking down the hall, seeing bullies giving others wedgies. Yet when walking by we choose not to interfere and do absolutely nothing. Some of us laugh. Some of us would want to do something, yet just can't find the courage. You might happen to be one of these bullies. Or the victim perhaps? I don't recall hearing anything about cutting your underpants before going to school. But if so, I'm sure they rip pretty easy. Are you tired of getting picked on and having to feel the pain from wedgies? Now, there is no need to worry! Have I got news for you! Introducing the new and improved Joe Boxer! Guaranteed NOT to give you wedgies.

Zest: Feeling dirty? Sorry, Zest doesn't clean feelings... Good bye dirt, grime and muck! Start running from Zest! Hello clean and smell good body. This is for everybody. By far the most powerful soap out on the market today! Also, available in different scents that will drive your senses crazy! Zest will have your body feeling smooth as a baby's bottom! That's right! Devouring all that roughness. So, after a hard day's work, are you working until your rear end fell off? Looks like it's still on to me! So, if you're feeling dirty - then try Zest, you'll end up becoming clean – just not as clean as when Jesus is done with yah!

Viagra: Introducing a new and improved... (What the!?) *CLICK*

Ooops Wrong Button! CAN YOU HEAR ME NOW? HOLD ON, GIVE ME A SECOND, LET ME TURN THE VOLUME BACK DOWN! *CLICK* That's better; let's see where was I... Oh yah, hopefully this is the right button. *CLICK* ..., ..., ..., Nope, hit the mute. *CLICK* There, that's more like it. Sorry about that, when it's dark sometimes I don't know what I'm *CLICKING* but at least you didn't need to hear about that advertisement. I have to say, some ads can be so deceiving. They lead us into the darkness if we buy into them. At times we choose to buy into them time after time. It's time to come out from that darkness and face the light. I could go on and on about the so called "fun" in regards to this and what it does to us or what it's already done. However, what's the point of that if you already know? Don't you want to be set free? No longer being a slave to that bondage? You might believe that you're not good enough and need to drink to "fit" in. You might believe it's the only thing to numb out the pain you're facing from a lost one or from being intimidated. Or possibly just to "feel" accepted. It has to be more of a reason than having so called "fun". I have come to find out it's not worth it and will no longer believe those lies in regards to it. If we choose to believe the lie for so long, it eventually starts to feel like the truth. At times we keep a little bit of ourselves hidden. Are we afraid, looking at ourselves for who we become and not for whom God made us? Deep down if we didn't like ourselves; we have no one to blame but ourselves. I now have real truth, in which Christ provides. Only through HIM can we be set free! He sees past the fakeness and searches our hearts! You don't have to live a life of curiosity that leads you down the wrong path. I'm writing this because I feel the pain of many out there and don't want them to take the same path that I once chose. Trust in Christ and take the road less traveled.

I urge you to stay connected to the main source! For instance, pretend that you're in the middle of a football game. Let's just say the teams are Alabama VS Iowa... "Roll Tide" as "Iowa Fights". If I chose to unplug this T.V. from its source of power, *CLICK* Then the screen dies. There is no life in the technology provided, no picture displayed and many become pissed off!!! Nooo!!! What the!? What if I told you, "Regardless of which fan you are, your team wins?" "How can you say that?" You might ask. I believe win or lose, as long as they play the game they love; giving it their all, full potential, heart and effort, you know their all in all... Then deep down inside they still win regardless of a loss. True sportsmanship congratulates the other wining team. If the T.V. stays connected to the source of power, *CLICK* then you'll come to find out and see that Alabama always wins. "ROLL TIDE!" Stay connected and focused on God as our source, His word prevails and light penetrates that darkness! The choices we make throughout the day, throughout the week are pretty vital. They affect the outcome of our lives, not only ours but also the others that live around us. Are we impacting those around us positively? Are we really concerned for their outcome of life? Do we want to see them succeed? Are we too busy focusing on ourselves that we can't see the big picture? You might ask, "So, what windows can we leave open in regards to impacting us in a positive way?" Well, I'm glad you asked.

I'm not sure why I need to come up with some of the answers here, I mean we all have brains and a conscience of whether it's right or wrong, good or bad... Here are a few windows that I choose to leave open and I hope these windows come your way. However, that would be a site to see. Right? I mean literally a window racing down the street, jumping into a gap between the exterior wooden trim. Here I am, open me! Anyways, I love building a relationship with God! Talking to Him on a daily basis, but also taking some time to listen to Him and follow through. After all, He inspired me and told me to open up my laptop and to start typing... So I did! Also, I love getting into God's word! Not just getting into it, really letting it come to life as the words jump off the page. Taking in what is said, having a more spiritual meaning behind it so I can actually apply His word in and through action. I have already mentioned a few in this book. Seeing the needs of others met before ours, loving and caring for our brothers with a passionate heart. Are we willing to make a stand when others choose to go down that same old road? In other words, holding others accountable out of love and respect, as well as ourselves. Even when times get tough, are we man enough to realize the gain of experience and understanding when we walk though rough situations that have an impact on us. We must choose to walk them out in the right manner. I know at times we still stumble and fall, but are we just going to stay there? A righteous man falls seven times, yet rises again! So in regards to what windows we choose to leave open, I urge you to decide wisely. We all are meant to rise and shine for God's Glory! We are children of light, adopted into his son ship! Arise and dust yourself off! Walk into the light and leave the darkness behind! Praise God! Thank You Jesus!!! So, in conclusion, any windows left open eventually become wide open doors that are hard to shut. Some doors may become useful, but make sure you are choosing the right doors. The left ones may tend to lead you astray. In today's news some are practicing the art of satanic worship... Ah, Man... I left the T.V. on *CLICK*

Chapter 05

The "Joy" Ride

I'm sure many of you can agree that most of us have some type of vehicle that gets us to our destination. As long as it gets us to point A & B and back again then for the most part that's really all we need. What about the rest of the alphabet though? C – Z... Can you even see through Z? And if you could, what would be on the other side? _____ Let's face it, at times when we are going to point B, we get sidetracked going to and from other places that wasn't even a part of our schedule in the first place. Anyways, for the most part we choose to just get in our vehicles and take off. We hardly ever check a few things before leaving if not check anything at all. Why not make sure the tires look good. Why not take some extra time to make sure there is enough oil in the engine? Perhaps even look at the gas gauge, making sure there is enough to arrive at our destination, making a round trip. It amazes me that sometimes we are stranded because the vehicle ran out of gas. On the other hand, we might have ran out of common sense to check the gas gauge in the first place... Oh, that's right it's broken. Yup that's why. Why not save enough money to actually fix a few things? Do people even save money any more or do we just blow it on whatever, whenever every second we get? What are we doing to go the extra mile in our lives, making sure what we drive is safe on the roads?

Have you ever thought that if our vehicle isn't safe to drive, then it could possibly damage others? And I'm not just talking about cars here. Let's face it; if we choose to drive on a low tire then the tire could burst, causing the driver to panic, pulling to the right and bam. We thought we were right to drive when we were left. Left feeling with emptiness after finding out that we just wrecked. Wrecked into what? Well, hard to say at this point. We have a lot to fix before getting back on the road. I'd have to say most people think of their own vehicle first, instead of wondering if the poor old squirrel is still alive that we just ran over. What if this wasn't a squirrel though? I'm sure you get the point even though its nuts... Thank God this is just a book, but hey; it could happen. So why not place some positive habits into effect? I personally make it a habit to fill my tank once it hits roughly around a quarter of a tank. I now also check my tires. I remember a time where I didn't check my tires before leaving. I'm so thankful for all the amazing people that help others out in life. Andy took some time to care, letting me know about the low tire. The final result could have been a lot worse.

In many ways cars operate and run similar to our own lives. The Bible talks about putting on the full armor of God. While driving, it's good to wear a seatbelt for safety, however many choose not to. Perhaps, those that choose not to wear the belt, have an extra one hundred dollars lying around? That could add up to a lot of copies of this book. I remember my first ticket, never again. Talk about a short term memory. Other than seatbelts, how are we placing safety into action? We might wear some goggles to protect our eyes. You might carry a can of pepper spray... Why not place a brick inside that purse? *WHACK* Now that would hurt, plus you get a work out! Safety is a form of protection. The engine needs oil to run and move properly. In a way, our body is kind of like an engine. Our body needs the proper nutrition throughout the day to function properly as well. If we choose not to eat we start to become weak. Also, I believe the muscle that we have is the first thing to go. However, it's not just the physical food that our body needs. The truth is that spiritual food is way more vital. If we eat some bad food, that might bring fourth some bad gas. Speaking of gas... If a car is low on gas, or perhaps out of gas, then it's not going anywhere and needs to be filled. Right now, I wouldn't be surprised if some were thinking, "Duh!" The same way a car uses gas to ignite a fire, allowing the engine parts to move properly, God's Spirit ignites us to fulfill His perfect will in our own lives.

God's Temple to His Holy Spirit, which is our body, is built on spiritual efforts. We need the Word of God in our lives so that we are filled with fuel to spark His Spirit, igniting the fire. Those words are full of life and power, more than just some black and white statements. As we read and choose believe, we are filled and must walk out His will by faith. When we hear God speak, we have an opportunity to move and act on it. Life, at times, hits just like when the rubber meets the road. It's important to have tires on any vehicle we choose to drive. It's pretty hilarious seeing a vehicle riding on nothing but bare rims. A couple of Cops episodes have filmed this. I'm sure you could YouTube it. Speaking of tubes, please take some time and check the tires. Make sure they are full of air, but not too full... otherwise they'll be likely to explode. And you don't want that to happen to your car. So, let's check out a few vehicles that you'll choose to drive. That's right! I'm letting you choose what type of vehicle you would like to drive. What's that? You'd rather walk? Yah, you look like you just might need the exercise. But then again, how would I know what you look like? That'd be kind of weird, wouldn't it? Anyways, to the garage, shall we?

THE GARAGE

As you know, the garage is like a home to a vehicle... To some, possibly even a type of living room man cave. I wouldn't be surprised to hear about some parties or band practices that take place in a garage. Our home is where we hang our hats as some might say. I personally don't wear hats, but to me it's important to have a clean house. I'm not sure how your home looks at this point, but wouldn't it be nice to walk into a clean and organized living space. I highly encourage you to take the time and effort to fulfill this. You might be stepping over things just to get to the couch or to your room. You might have just done this before reading. If so, it's ok... I can assure you this book will not vanish into thin air. Go ahead and take some time to clean up your quarters. No, I'm not talking about change here either silly. Unless, however, it's a positive change by living this out. All clean? Yes, No... We'll it's your choice. We can either accept the advice given or throw it on the ground! You can't say maybe either, because you'll either do it or you won't. Anyways, I don't have an electronic garage door opener so this might take awhile...

Ugh! This garage door is heavy. Give me a hand will yah? Thanks! It's good to have friends by your side willing to lend you a helping hand. Do you recall the last time you've helped someone? Wait, you already did. I'm not talking about the garage door either. I mean, you purchased this book didn't you? Well, you might actually be reading it free of charge. If so, it's all good! I just want to reach some lives out there. It's awesome to touch and speak truth into others lives! I hope a passionate heart develops inside all of you as well. Don't miss out on the opportunities that pass us by. At times, we allow them to pass us. Do you wonder what would have happened if you had said yes? This goes far beyond living in a clean house. When the time comes, take a chance, risk a few minutes out from our busy schedules just to see what happens. I myself am taking a risk in not only writing this book, but letting you drive one of these cars. Let me help you choose what vehicle you'd like to drive by giving a basic rundown on each one. Since there are so many cars out there, I'm narrowing it down between an import and a muscle car. Whatever car is not chosen, I'll have my twin drive that for the day. Sorry bro, you're along for the ride.

It would be kind of difficult to travel in both vehicles. I'm pretty sure not every reader will choose the same car. On the other hand, I could have a split personality... You might see that in your own life or possibly someone else's. Do we tend to act one way around people we love, only trying to get something from them or even to draw attention to ourselves? Do we then act a totally different way in front of others? In the long run, when we do this, it's not only eating us up on the inside... No, it's much worse. It actually tends to affect the others around us as well. Let's think about it. If they actually knew the real you would they lose heart? Would they still want to hang out with you? Are you afraid of what others might think or say if they actually knew the real you? God sees past all the counterfeit identities we tend to maintain. God examines and searches our hearts. He truly perceives us for who we are and destined to be. He desires us to reclaim the identities we once lost. We no longer need to act a certain way around others just to get them to like us. If anyone can't accept you for who you are, then truly they are not a friend. I challenge us to take the masks off that we have allowed ourselves to wear time and time again. Let our true personality shine as it's drawn into the light, breaking away from the darkness. Speaking of shine, I just waxed this vehicle and I got to say, it's beaming.

Alright, first up we have "The Black Widow"! Its stunning appearance will have heads turn as you switch lanes while the paint drips! It's also got a smoking sound system that carries for about a six block radius. If that's not loud enough for yah, it's fast and furious with a mean bite leaving other racers stranded in the dust. This import comes fully equipped with all the special modifications including a full tank of NOS! You'll have no problem seeing that checkered flag in your rear view!

Next up, we have "The Rusted Ol' Clunker". This muscle car might not sound like much, but she's a bute! This rust bucket still starts and takes off with no problems. This classic actually comes with the original eight track player! So, if you're in the mood for some old time hits, this is the ride for you! But wait! That's not all!!! It's decomposing as rust eats away at its side fenders. In fact, a piece just fell off last week! You know it's guaranteed to make some heads turn!!!

Regardless of what vehicle you decide, life is a beautiful ride. At times we go through the motions; the highs and the lows. Through the trials and testing we face, we gain experience, understanding, knowledge and a whole lot more... Do we tend to buckle under pressure? At times, we need to be broken in order to be built. When we walk out our struggles with a hope, knowing God provides, this produces perseverance. We then have the strength to persevere through the trial, which produces character after we face the battle and succeed! I would like to see all of us succeed in life. I would especially like to see you succeed far and beyond myself. This goes for even the ones that you, yourself have interacted with from time to time. You might not feel the same way, but that's ok. I just know that if it wasn't for God saving me from myself, I wouldn't have a life. Choosing to lay down my life for God, consist of sacrificing time as well. Time to do His will and not our own. I know I chose my own way at one point in time... I thank God he woke me up, answering my prayers, hearing my cry. Well, it's beginning to be about that time. Let's Ride!!!

(Please turn to the page based on your vehicle selection located in this same chapter)

THE BLACK WIDOW

Alright! You chose the rice burner, and no it doesn't actually burn rice. I suppose you could if you placed some either on the engine or at the back of the muffler though... Where's the keys? Oh, yah... Here you go! Let's start it up! VOOOMM... Hmm *clank*clank*clank*clank*clank* Hmm... You might be wondering what that sound is. Due to some wear and tear, it might be normal. Then again, there is no normal. What would that even look like anyway? We all have different gifts and talents, we don't dress alike, some of us are tall, or skinny... I could go on and on. Anyways, even though this vehicle sure is attractive, it's been used quite a bit. Does that ever happen in your life? Do we sometimes use others because of what they have or what they can do for us? Do we even allow others to use us? Many times we choose to say, "Yes" instead of "No" just because we are intimidated about what others would do. We worry about the final results when they haven't even come into play yet. I challenge you to take an extra step, having some boldness, not allowing others to walk all over you in life. It seems as if this car was pretty much "walked" on after hearing all the spitting noises and such. Are we taking care of the stuff we purchase in life? Or when something needs fixed, do we just throw it away? And why did it need fixed in the first place? Most of the time, if we would choose to place our heart into the things we have and actually take care of things, they would not break so easily or so fast. We are all called to be good stewards of what God blesses us with. Everything that we have should be taken care of, to make last. I know, you're probably wondering, "Let's test drive this thing already." Right? Well, then... Let's Go!

Ok, from the Garage, we'll go right... Right to the Interstate to put this puppy in top gear! I'm sure you notice at times some choose to drive pretty slow when it comes to taking an on ramp onto the interstate. By the time we are exiting the ramp we should be going about the same speed posted on the freeway. I'm sure many times people are furious when they are behind others that choose to drive like 40 – 60 mph while they arrive onto the freeway. I wonder... Maybe they call it interstate because we "enter" other states. However, I'm not sure why they call it a freeway, when it's not the "free" way. I mean, we still have to pay for gas to even be on it and for that matter we can't go as fast as we want when a sign is posted that says "Speed Limit". Then again, others could be taking precaution, perhaps having a baby on board. Nope, I know... they might be talking on their cell phone, losing focus because they are more into the conversation than the actual driving. Maybe, it's a senior citizen... however, not all seniors are slow behind the wheel. I personally know a couple myself. We think or choose to say, "Out of the way Grandma!" Or, I have to admit, we do at times say things that are much worse. Ok, let's hit the fast lane!!

When we choose to live life in the fast lane, we miss out on things... possibly rush to get things done, in which it most likely turns out all sloppy. We don't take our time, losing accuracy in our position. We need to take a breather at times and not get so much into a hurry. It's good to stay at a steady productive pace. If we choose to slow things down too much, then we are just dragging along. This can affect others around us as well, possibly getting rear ended and throwing us off the map. I'm not just talking about driving here. Even during our work hours, we should work diligently and effectively. This could consist of staying a bit later, putting in some overtime to insist that things get done. That's effective, productive and has some sort value to the company. I want to encourage everyone out there to place their heart and effort into their jobs. Many people don't have jobs at this moment. How would you feel if they took your position? If you knew that they were about to, would this make you work a little harder or at least be a little more serious in the position that you have. So, as we accelerate up to about 140mph we need to make quick reactions. *SWERVE* ohhh... Man! Watch Out!! *SWERVE* Driving super fast is dangerous! Swerving to the left, to the right, dodging other cars and trucks is pretty crazy. I mean, one small mistake and *BAM* it's over! It's not like a video game where we can restart at the on ramp or even start where we left off at. No, we would have to start at the hospital, possibly learning how to do things all over again. This is serious stuff. What was I talking about again? Oh yah, some choose not to take things seriously. Trust me, I know... Sometimes we have to learn the hard way. Oh, man! We need to get to a gas station fast. Take the next off ramp and head toward downtown; otherwise we'll be following through, learning the hard way by walking to get some gas.

Screeching to a halt, we arrive at the station. Fill er' up! Remember what I stated earlier about gas? We need to add Premium to this bad boy! Why not a little dose of high octane additive as well? God fills us up, just like the fuel is used to start a car. The fuel is used to get all the parts moving, getting us to our destination and hopefully making it back again. When God fills us, we have opportunities to pour into the lives of others as well as completing his perfect will. After we pour out, speaking truth into others and helping them achieve and be successful; we can at times feel drained, yet full of Joy to seek God and start the cycle all over again! It's great being an open vessel, allowing God to use us for His Glory! $60 Dollars!? Gas prices are pretty crazy now-a-days. It's best to save and plan accordingly to what the open road leaves ahead of us. Toward downtown we can be easily distracted by advertisement signs, bars, gentlemen clubs, etc... Speaking of which, curiosity kicks in and wonders about the small red button. NOooo!!! *PRESS* Curiosity can be a dangerous at times, choosing to follow through into the unknown. We later come to realize that the unknown became known; either in a good or bad way. At least we sometimes have the option to learn from our mistakes. That small red button came to be known as shooting a tank of NOS into the engine! As we drive in the fast lane… "Ohhh SNAPS!" Hold on to your ______! = //\V/\V/\V/ *CRASH*

(Please turn page to "Destination Beautiful" located at the end of this chapter)

THE RUSTED OL' CLUNKER

Alight! You chose the rusted old muscle car that seems to have no muscle at all! Grab a crow bar will yah? We need to get this hood open to check the oil first. Just give it a little love tap. *CLANK* Oh, man! Not so hard! I didn't expect that to happen... Part of the front bumper just fell off. Oh well, at least we got the hood open. WOW, check this out! The engine is a brand new 350 small block with all the special modifications. This pushes it to about 550hp at 6300rpm! I bet you didn't expect that under the hood did yah? Many times we tend to judge others by their looks. God cares more about the heart, not the appearance. We don't need to dress to impress. When living for Him, it's about placing the gospel into action. It's about caring and loving our brothers, sisters, friends, family... People we know, people we don't know. It's about following through with what He informs us to do. For instance, if I chose not to follow through with what the Father informed me, you would have not been able to read the last two chapters due to the fact that it wouldn't even exist. Are there any moments you, yourself missed out on that would exist if you would have chose to follow through? Think about it, you wouldn't even be reading these words right now. It would be like a blank page, with no life, inspiration, thought, or affection. Would you still have bought it? A book with a bunch of blank pages and a series of underscores... Could possibly be a journal I suppose? Hmmm, maybe I should add a couple of blank pages in this book. Since I've been writing, God has already been touching lives as others read the book He inspired me to write and it's not even published yet! Wait, it will be or already has depending on when you're reading this... We are the ones that put limits on God. God has no limits; there is no end to what a living God can do in and through us. I want to encourage you to open up your heart to Him, allowing Him to overflow, pouring Joy into your life. Ready to ride it out?

Let's start this puppy up shall we? VOOOAAAMMM!!! hhHHMMmmMMMmm - Ahh... Purring like a kitten. Now that's the cat's meow! What's up with all those animal sounds anyway? I mean we went from puppy, to kitten, and now cat. What about the cow's moo? Or the bird's tweet, the mouse squeak, the dogs woof, the horses nay – I mean hay... I'm sure you get the sound. Why don't we put this lion into gear and roar! Ok, from the Garage we'll go left... leaving the suburbs while heading straight into the open road. Ahhh, the open road. Don't you just love taking a joy ride on the highway sometimes? I mean with today's gas prices I can understand why not. I remember many moments just cruising around driving nowhere, which I'm now here. Honestly, I can't afford driving around for fun anymore. When I head out, I usually tend to make sure I stop at all the places I need to, stocking up on the bare necessities. Bears stock up on tons of food and water before hibernation yah know. It's good to plan ahead; otherwise we tend to wing it. We go about our day with our feet on the ground and our heads in the clouds. Sure, this is possible. Have you ever walked through fog? It's like we can only see so far ahead of us, not knowing where we are going at times. It's crucial to see where you are heading; walking out the goals and plans you have in life. If you don't have a plan, you plan to fail. It just might so happen that we might fall off a cliff, walking in the midst of a foggy night. Also, a goal without a plan is just a wish. Following through with a plan is a good habit to get into. This way you're consistently not driving on a daily basis wasting not only time, but money burning from your gas tank. What's that!? Actual money burning in your gas tank! Stop the car!!! *EXPLODE!* You know what I'm talking about! I "wish" I would have done that... I "wish", I "wish", I "wish". If you had three wishes you might as well wish for more. It's time to rise up and actually place those plans in action!

Saying, "Yes", this is more important and this needs to get done! No Regrets!!! Place the rubber to the road! "Let's GO!!!" I'm pretty hungry at this moment. Aren't you? Want to get something to eat? It's ok, you can place this book down and mark it you know?

What are you hungry for? Let's go pick up a six pack and a pound! Huh? What's that? Oh, Yeah! Let me come across this a little more clearly. Words can be so deceiving at times. On one hand, this could mean a six pack of beer and a pound of marijuana! I mean, we did just got off from the "high"way . A man who stands on toilet is high on pot. On the other hand, if you have ever gone through the drive thru at Taco Johns, you would come to realize that this means a six pack of tacos and a pound of potato oles! OLE!!! It's like we want it right now, living in this microwave generation. Hardly any of us have any patience any more. Doesn't anyone like surprises anymore? I believe good things come to those who patiently wait. Most are like, no... If I had any more patients I'd be a doctor. What If you were told that if you could wait patiently for one week without eating meat? After that one week you would be rewarded with a nice Filet Mignon! Would you be able to do it? This obviously wouldn't work for vegetarians, but sure... Have some bacon wrapped around it as well. Furthermore, if we choose to wait patiently overnight to make a purchase, some of us actually would save a little bit of money realizing that they don't necessarily need the product. Why not wait until the price drops as well? Heck, you might have gotten a good deal on this book... Would you wait patiently at this stop sign before heading towards downtown? OLE!!!

As we approach downtown we come to a stop light. Yup, we are making heads turn alright! In fact, the driver that's to our right is saying something out from his window. Let's listen to what he has to say. "Look at that rusted old piece of junk!" "I bet you that's slow enough to drive Miss Daisy!" "If I kick it, would the wheels fall off?"

"Nope, just the side fender, possibly the whole bumper!" At times, we don't know when to quit and keep edging each other on until some steam forms, enough to boil some tea. Having a tea party are we? Let's see... "I'll leave you in the dust and you'll be eating my bumper literally!" "How's that rust taste now!" "Seems like you could use the iron anyway!" So now we have to prove our point and finish something that's been started. I have to say the better man is the one who ends the conversation by walking away, not fighting. Others might think differently, then calling them names, trying to take it even further. It's not worth it and we don't have to prove anything. It's best to get rid of our pride by finding the lie behind why we have to express it. Does it make you feel like a better person? Are we just not humble enough to walk away and have to face the consequence of what happens? So as we take off, we are neck and neck realizing that a car is in front of us. We have two choices. We can either be stupid enough to pass on the left hand side, heading straight into oncoming traffic. Or, we can give up and let the other person win. Being all prideful, wanting to prove something, we choose to pass on the left. Bad move! "Ohhh SNAPS!" Hold on to your _____! = \\V/\V/\V/\\ *CRASH*

(Please turn page to "Destination Beautiful" located at the end of this chapter)

Destination Beautiful 53

Destination Beautiful

Death is a destination that we all come across at some point in time. However, at this point, I'm sure you are not dead. If that were true, you wouldn't be reading this at the moment. So what comes to my mind at this moment is how are we personally living our lives? If you knew you had 24 hours to live, what would you change? What would you do? Hopefully you just wouldn't waste your life away. I mean, if so, do you really have a passion to do nothing? We must have some type of strong drive in our lives in order to steer us on the path to our destiny. What are we allowing ourselves to be influenced with that moves us in the direction we take? I mean, it's our choice... We choose to make it, we choose to take it. This plays a huge role in our destination, not by chance or a roll of some dice either. We must be responsible for our actions, either good or bad. Speaking of action...

This just in! Breaking News!!! An old rusted piece of garbage was totaled in a head on collision today. At this point, it's hard to make out what both of the vehicles were. However, police are saying the phrase "Black Widow" was found on one of the pieces all scattered across the street. By the looks of the wreckage it doesn't seem as if anyone survived. Yup, word just in, some bodies were found in the rubbish, clearly wiped off the face of this earth to a point of no return. May God bless their souls? How are we living? What choices are we choosing to do, not realizing the consequences that we must face are ahead of us? I can assure you, life is no "Joy" ride when it comes down to having so called fun. We try to do, find, or even buy things to give us a lasting joy, not realizing its only happiness. Happiness only lasts for a short time. Yet, Joy... Joy comes straight from God as we fulfill His will. Joy lasts for eternity, filling us up when we are left empty. God has a perfect plan for each and every one of us. We must choose to do what the Father has in store for us. I urge you to take the road less traveled. It's a narrow road, narrow enough only to fit people. I can assure you that no cars fit on this road. I have a tendency for this message to impact many out there. Be advised that no matter what road we choose, they all lead to the same destination. No one escapes the final judgment seat of Christ.

Chapter 04

Reader's Block

In some cases, writers develop some type of block where they can't think of what to write. But what about the reader's? Are we blocked out from reality? Are we trapped inside a dream? Do we choose to place these ideas, goals, and examples into action? I admit, sometimes no ideas come to mind, but I believe there are many ideas that are not even developed yet. Many are out there trapped in a mind, just waiting to be exposed, set free, and invented. Free your mind and be encouraged to never stop dreaming! I say, regardless of the idea, mention it. The only dim ideas are the ones not lit. Bright ideas may take a while to develop and form to become a part of reality, but we must never give up. Sometimes we hide behind fear, believing that others will not like it or possibly think it's stupid. We are left, choosing to believe a lie that hasn't even developed yet. And, so what if some think it's stupid... I wouldn't be surprised if some didn't even like this book, but as you can see that will not stop me from typing. I encourage you to stand out! Be bold and courageous, standing firm on the solid foundation, in which you believe in. Stay firmly planted so that when trials and tribulations come it won't break the ground, pulling us apart, leaving us in a state of confusion. Be encouraged to help others by leading them, not being intimidated by fear, but empowered with love! Are you ready to change, becoming some type of building block? Or would you rather just stay blocked?

What's blocking us from actually taking a step forward to try something new? What's stopping us from pushing forth the ideas and goals into practice, bettering our lives? What do you feel after reading the following? At times, dreams can seem to be so real. Other times they can actually form into reality, sort of creating like a dajavu moment. Has that ever happened to you? I say in-between those meanings is like being trapped in a coma. We are in a state of sub consciousness, in which dreaming seems like a different reality. It seems like everywhere we turn, we eventually hit a wall and yet can't find an exit. Are we blocked? Are we trapped? I can assure you there is a way out. Even at times it might seem as if we took a dead end, yet if so... most of the time we just turn around and go back the way we came. I wonder what would happen if we chose to plow through that dead end? I'm sure some type of conclusion would develop after a break through occurs. After starting, it's like trying to finish a complex maze. Yet what if that maze didn't have a finish? You would eventually have to come back to the start. Are you now blocked? Let's go back to the start. So, you're back at the start. In some cases, writers develop some type of block where they can't think of what to write. But what about the reader's? Wait, I just stated this in the first sentence... You decide to keep on reading; however you do have a choice not to enter that same maze without a finish. Since I'm the author, does that make me to come up with the only means of escape? Sure you could just put down the book, making an exit to take the easy way out... But, if that were the case this book would end here. Not here.

Are you still reading? If I answered yes, would I be wrong? I guess that depends on if you are still reading. And if I was wrong, how many wrongs would I have to make to make it right? Wrong, wrong, wrong... Nope, it's still sounds wrong. Yet at times, it seems like we do things wrong long enough to where it just starts to "feel" right. By all means, get rid of those lies! We need to rise up and face our problems. At times we develop walls to "block" out reality, not wanting to deal with our issues that come our way. We allow these problems to control us, instead of us coming up with solutions to solve the problems. I mention "reader's block" because, I myself, am reading this as I type. Since I am reading this as I type, am I blocked as well? I have to admit, I haven't even reached the full potential of whom I'm created to be. This is a never ending process. There is always something new to learn, to discover, and to place into action. This is true not only for my life, but for yours as well. Many of us find ourselves blocked at times, not willing to change. We choose to run away from our problems instead of facing them head on! We come up with excuses to block out the picture instead of dealing with our issues. While watching T.V., many of us would say something if another person stepped in front of our view. So why don't we do the same when it comes down to other "issues". I wonder if any of the readers are actually taking to heart what is mentioned or if they have become "blocked". I have to admit that at times, I myself, don't take advise right way. At times I used to stay in that blocked state. It's like waiting at a toll booth, digging and searching for change before you can cross over. There are many books out there that give out tons of advice. However, the final result always finishes off with this simple fact; it's up to us to decide. It's choices we either choose to receive or reject. Its advice we either choose to accept or ignore. If we choose to accept it, it's up to us to follow through and place it into action! If we choose to ignore it and not take a risk at times, where does that leave us? Does that leave us back to the start?

In some cases, writers develop some type of block where they can't think of what to write. But what, but what about, but what about.... Wait, didn't we just read this? You could relate this to a CD that's all covered up with scratches. And believe you me, you don't want that. You might as well toss that out the window. Has that window become a door? By the way, I think it's cool that Chapter 4 is actually the fourth chapter. If we chose not to take a risk and place advice into action, then yes, it's like not even reading this book at all. It's like wasting our valuable time as we read some information that becomes worthless. Is it possible to put a price on information? I mean, information is practically everywhere we go. It's the facts on the side of candy bars, it's signs that we drive past every day, it's reports that we come across in a newspaper or on T.V. There is so much about information. It's even signs of warning, in which at times we choose to ignore that as well. Why are we so curious to pay no attention to warnings? At times, we follow through, passing over the warning line. With curiosity in mind, in a way we become a part of that caution to begin with. At times we overlook truth considering a way that we'd rather prefer, which leads to figuring it out on our own. Most of the time, this refers to figuring a way out from the mess we dug ourselves into. Are we afraid to accept advice? Are we afraid of asking for help? Does this make you feel like you're weak? Let me help you with this one, unless you'd like to keep on reading about being stuck in a coma? I'll mention more about this later, but first here... Take my hand; let's escape back to a state of consciousness, bringing the reality back into words.

This is a state of reality, regardless of which state you are in. A series of underscores eventually becomes a line, which we all know lines can form and create things. So multiple lines together can form objects, which put together properly creates... well pretty much anything. So you might ask if, we ourselves are a series of underscores. Nope, I just thought that would be something cool to say. However, since a series of underscores can create lines, we all know lines can create letters. Letters placed in the right order produces words, which then words become sentences to produce information. We choose buy into information all the time, yet we ourselves are priceless. We all were bought at a price in which no form of money could ever buy. God loves us so much, more than we could ever know. It's by His grace we are saved. Jesus sacrificed himself while we were still sinners so that a way could be made. Are you tired of living "your" way? I know I was. My life was pointless without God. Just meaningless! I've come to realize that to have His plan unfold; we must choose to play our part in His design! We must get past the statements where it's all about me. We must choose to step outside of "ourselves". Truth is it's all about God. He's alive and took time crafting the perfect design for each and every one of us. We choose to mess that up by going our own way, abusing our freewill. Are we using or misusing our freedom? If you "miss" using your freedom, then why are you trapped? At times we focus on the things we can't do more than on the things that we can do. When our focus is like that, we become miserable! Let's face it; if I choose to not follow a blueprint of a building, then I just might need to crawl through the window in order to get inside. The dimensions and lines are in the perfect spots on those blueprints. This goes far beyond building a home too. I'm talking about setting a firm foundation, a solid structure for our lives. We need to take a serious aim on how we are building our lives.

Sometimes we see how close to the line we can get, then realize we took a step past that line and are on the other side. When others are willing to lend a helping hand trying to pull us back on the right path, we choose to cut the rope traveling further and farther away, being lead astray... We can only help those who are willing to be helped. Why do we tend to cross the line sometimes anyway? Are we forming an x or possibly a t? Hopefully you just didn't read that as the word at. It's meant to say or possibly a tee, as in the letter t. If we cross the line to form a cross, then by all means cross it! It's awesome that God defeated the enemy using 3 nails and a cross. If we cross the line to form an x, then x marks the spot just like on a treasure map. In this case, many have a curiosity of wondering what the x might reveal. Some gold perhaps? We would go the distance, possibly doing anything just to dig up what is buried. However, if that x leads to some treasure of knowledge, understanding, and experience... most wouldn't even bother taking the risk. We wouldn't even think about traveling the distance to acquire useful skills for our lives. This is somewhat similar to how the enemy pulls our strings. This is not some puppet show either.

The enemy loves to deceive us. He doesn't dress up in red, having a tail and horns. He disguises himself as an angel of light. We are drawn into things that look so pleasing and pleasurable to the eye. When drawn in, the enemy separates us from the truth. This allows lies to sink in. We believe the lies, follow through and are lead astray. The message becomes unclear. It's no longer plain and simple. It's no longer black and white. He turns darkness into light, and light into darkness. So what's wrong just feels right. By light, I mean the truth, honesty, peace, compassion, real love. By darkness, I mean the lies, misery, sorrow, hopelessness, selfishness, manipulation, pride, anger, etc... We are deceived into believing that God is the source of darkness. While we saturate ourselves in that darkness disguised as light, we eventually wind up in a state of distress. Yet in the midst of that, we tend to focus all our hate toward the only One that can save us. I can assure you that God didn't place us in that darkness. We, ourselves, chose to go that route. We choose to cross over into the unknown to make known. We are lead astray, arriving at that state by our own freewill. I want to encourage you to stay on the right path and carry out the will God has in store for you. Be truthful and honest. Have compassion for one another. Create peace and accept one another, just as Christ accepted you.

God has a perfect plan. He has a perfect will for each and every one of us. When we carry that out, we still face trials and tribulations of many kinds. Even though we still face problems, He is there and wants to help. He provides us with so much, wanting to see us succeed. When we walk through trials and testing in the right manner, we receive a prize. Yippee! A PRIZE!!! Some believe that this prize is more along the line of winning the lottery or receiving a free car. You get a prize alright! However, we can't drive or fly it. We can't spend it, or even at times see it. What we can do, though, is feel it. We feel it deep down inside with confirmation from God's Holy Spirit. We further develop our character; gaining courage, strength, and boldness. We further develop moral fiber. Mmmm... Fiber! This goes far beyond good food. I believe many of us have different meanings to that phrase. To me, it's not afraid to go after what's most important. It's expressing your love for one another, telling the truth regardless if it hurts. It's loving someone enough to mention that they are meant for so much more. It's seeing others for who they really are, when others don't realize who they are. It's voicing out reality, making it easier to distinguish between putting on a show and just plain being real. We advance our lives increasing the amounts of experience, knowledge, and understanding! We are equipped with tools for the right jobs!

Why don't we use these tools to even further develop others in life, not just focusing on ourselves? Seriously! Would you use a torch to hang a picture? Well, the picture is hung... but the house in on fire! Hopefully our insurance covers insanity. Daily, we have opportunities to stand out. Daily, we have time after time to make things right with one another. Daily we have chance after chance to bless someone by pouring into their lives. We have opportunities to uplift our brothers and sisters as well. This goes far much deeper than family too. I'm talking about everyone that is around us. We interact with others on a daily basis throughout our busy schedules. Go ahead, try something new! Have a conversation with a stranger or even an employee that you hardly spend enough time with. We can impact so many, placing a huge piece of the puzzle back into alignment. We, ourselves, just might be that missing piece. We can choose to be a unit, using what we have and are blessed with to help change this world. It's all about choice. We could choose not to change at all, yet I'm sure most of you can agree this is still a choice.

The choices we make dictate the life that we lead. The bad things we might have gotten away with in the past will eventually catch up with us. In the mean time we feel regret, remorse, and resentment from doing things we know that we shouldn't. If we choose to help others be successful as well, then we feel joyful. We have a sense of hopefulness, knowing that we are designed and created for a purpose. I want to encourage all of you to be serious about life, knowing where you are heading. Attempt to help others succeed and achieve their goals. Strive to become leaders! Why are we at times afraid to become leaders? Why do we feel intimidated, driven by fear? At times we don't risk in taking a step forward, panicking, thinking something will go wrong when it hasn't even happened yet. This all had to start from somewhere? I mean we just didn't wake up one day thinking, "I just want to ruin my life today." That sounds like a brilliant idea! Let's get serious for a moment. I mean, it has to come from something somewhere. That "something" I know only God can reveal when we truly trust in him. Let's take a trip back to the start. I'd like to mention a few things. And no, I won't be starting with the "writer's block" statement either...

Growing up as a child, not only living in the areas we were raised, but dealing with situations that occurred around us has a huge impact. Those situations play vital roles in developing who we have become today. Children need someone to look up to in life. They need positive role models to hang out with. Kids actually mimic what they see more than we know. I'm sure if parents acted out being true leaders, then as a child grows they would become one too. I'm not talking about putting on a show by being fake either. I'm talking about being genuine. If parents choose to fight in front of their children, then believe it or not the child usually grows up with traits acquired from that. They can become scared, thinking nothing can be done to correct this. They can tend to even grow up violent, causing pain into the lives of others. Do we take time explaining to them what the fight was all about? Do we show love and compassion to our children when they need it the most? Children even mimic what we do. Are we setting good examples, following through in action? Children see through their eyes, witnessing the things we do. If we choose to help our children with their homework, well then they not only get it done with better understanding. They also can develop a state of mind in understanding that homework is more important than watching movies or playing video games. Children repeat the words and phrases they hear. What are we saying around our children? Do we think it's cute when a child uses bad language? Are we, ourselves, training them properly? I thank God I no longer think the way I used to. Children desperately need some type of positive influence as their lives develop. It's up to us, as the leaders, as the role models to become men of courage. We need to take a stand and care! It's time to stop family curses from being passed down to generation to generation. We need to be bold, not allowing thoughtless acts to control the entrance into our homes. We are the leaders! What are we doing to guide others, showing them the proper way? It's up to us to impact others leaving behind a Godly legacy!

True leaders actually lead by example. Don't you want your children as well as others around us to have some type of positive legacy? Hopefully we don't wake up thinking, "I really hope my son robs a bank or brings home an "F" today on his report card." What if your child does actually come home with an "F" on their report card? I hope we have some type of sense to care. What would we place into action to correct it? Hopefully this would not involve some type of spanking. I believe there are many of other ways to place discipline into action without having the need for violence. Instead of abusing our children, why not take away the T.V. for a couple weeks? Even better, what about dessert? This is a harsh punishment, I know. No chocolate caramel ice cream with whip cream on top. What about the sprinkles!? Mmm sprinkles... How about taking their cell phones away? I personally didn't own a trac-phone until I was about 27 years old. As a matter of fact, it was given to me. Nowadays, I believe many spend way too much time on their cell phones anyway. There has to be some type of discipline involved or most likely they will never learn. They do learn, however, to manipulate their way out of things. We as parents or leaders should be in control. The student should never walk all over the teacher. It's like a student coming into a chemistry class saying, "I got this!" "Move aside!" As he just starts mixing things together... *BOOOM!* An explosion happens and the next thing we know, we are running to the bathroom changing our pants. We'll, at least some type of "change" happened in this situation! We need to put our foot down at times, letting them know we mean what we say.

If we ourselves are not following through with what we say, then how can we expect others to carry it out? We become hypocritical, wearing masks... Seriously, how many masks can one wear? I have heard the saying, "He's a man of many talents." What about "The Mask"? For the most part, it's just being two faced. We act one way in front of family, then act totally different way behind closed doors. Had enough? *SLAM* Why don't we just go back to the start? In some cases, writers develop some type of block where they can't think of what to write. But what about the reader's? I mean seriously, as we read are we thinking... "Oh, yes... that's a really good statement; I should follow through with that." At times, we tend to take a mental picture of what we could do, yet we never actually follow through with it. Our lives stay at the same state and never develop any further. I personally have lived in many states. I've moved around so many times, I can't even give you a number. It's not because I can't count that high; I just don't keep a track record of it. Anyways, back to the point. It's up to us to make some type of commitment! We need to develop a mindset on being devoted to change. No one can force you to change, we decide. What if someone did force you? I'm sure you would eventually fight back or least, when no one is looking, you would go back to your original state. There would be no improvement. There would be nothing gained, just some type of collision as the final result.

What good is it to read a book and get nothing out from it? We choose to leave the information on the page! How worthless! We burn ourselves, not the book. I hope some don't actually tear the page out from the book either. That's not what I'm talking about. So, by now if you're still reading, I truly hope that some thoughts and ideas have come to your mind to place into action. I would like for these ideas not only to improve and impact your own life, but others as well. I believe it's good to help others reach their goals and see them succeed far and beyond ourselves. If others out there think the same way, they would eventually help you as well. Before going on to chapter three, I highly suggest that you come up with some goals to write down. Don't just write them down either; really strive to place them into action. So are you willing to take a risk, or possibly stay blocked from turning to the next chapter? It's your choice. I can't make you write anything. I can't force you to follow through. However, I can challenge you to turn the page. Do you dare? Sure you could turn the page without writing anything down, but that would just defeat the purpose.

Chapter 03

How Great Thou Art!

Believe it or not, forms of art are all around us. In fact, this sentence is one right now. Why not add another? This one is as well too. I truly believe that some type of gift or talent dwells deep down inside all of us. So deep to where some have yet to discover what their true gifts and talents are. If so, I want to encourage you to never give up. Never lose hope! Be confident; determine to uncover what's hidden in the dark by exposing it into the light. At times this could be a process of stepping outside ourselves from what we know. Experiment by trying something new, something different regardless of what others might think, say, or do. When I first started drawing, I didn't know how to draw. I just picked up a pencil and started doodling. This took time, effort, and patience placed into practice. It was the process of doing something unknown to make known. Overtime, I found it enjoyable regardless of what others thought. When I first experimented with drawing abstract designs, some did not like the final product. Some even mentioned it was stupid or they just didn't "get" it. If I chose to quit drawing because of what others thought, that talent would have never grown into the condition of where it's at today. Do we quit placing our heart and effort into projects because of what others think? Do we, ourselves, think that it's retarded to finish what was started? We can't set how strong our gifts are based by what others think. Also, we shouldn't think badly about our gifts that haven't even hit reality yet. Even though I never gave up drawing, I can admit at first some of the drawings produced were not very edifying.

What are we using our gifts and talents for? Do we tend to use our gifts only for ourselves? If so, why? Why not bless another person out there by using how God designed and created you to be. I challenge you to do so! You never know who you might inspire or lift up just to brighten someone's day. The gifts and talents that are implanted in our lives ought to be used to inspire others, to help others succeed, and mostly bring Glory to God. I truly believe if we choose not to use the gifts and talents God has blessed us with for His Glory, then He will find someone else that is willing. He will bless those that are willing to say "YES" in their hearts. From personal experience, I had a tendency to draw what the flesh desired. I drew unedifying hand gestures relating to throwing up the middle finger. By no means am I doing this now. I'm sure many readers would most likely throw this book at me. Anyway, back to the drawing board. I drew marijuana leaves and other drug related items. Most of the time, I was actually under the influence of drugs and thought that this was where I acquired my talent from. I was deceived into believing this lie. I thought that I needed to be high in order for my true gift to be drawn out, producing something different. As time when on, I knew that I was being stripped from my gift. What was produced resulted in pointless creations. Drawing doodles evolved into a complete mess. Eventually, no ideas struck my mind. It would be kind of similar to ending this book right now by typing a bunch of random statements. The fish jumped over the fence. I was unhappy with the results and I was wasting the gift in which God gave me.

It's vital not to waste the gifts and talents we have in our lives. We must choose to use them wisely. Many opportunities are around us daily, giving us chance after chance to engage. Since reading the last chapter, I wonder if you have placed any goals into action. Are you on the right track? Speaking of being on the right track, have you ever watched a train go by? I'm sure most could agree that when we are stopped in a vehicle, staring at a train is quite boring. Just imagine it. I wouldn't be surprised if some reading wouldn't want to. A line full of dull carts traveling on a track: Cart, Cart, Cart... How Boring!! Wait a second... OOoooo Look at that! Something pops out at you grabbing your attention. That something is usually graffiti, unless someone tried running the tracks, plowing straight into the train. Some refer to graffiti as a form of vandalism. However, I believe this is an amazing form of art which could be used for a powerful purpose. Think about it! Instead of having a bunch of dull carts pass us by, wouldn't it be nice to have some type of advertisement? Possibly some type of short clip? I believe many would not mind waiting for a train if something more than a bunch of plain dull old carts were striking their attention. At times we look at the negative side of things, not realizing the possibilities for positive outlooks. We tend to focus on what we can't do, rather than what we can do. Even though at times we dig ourselves into a pit full of junk, God sees past the turmoil. He truly sees the beauty in us for who we are destined to be.

We were formed from the dust on this earth, breathing His breath of life in us! Talk about an awesome Creator! He is the potter and we are the clay. I mean, haven't you ever seen some clay animated movies? It's crazy how sometimes clay can actually talk back to the potter. I admit some don't like the way they were created, so they find other ways to block out the pain. In all reality, we are destroying the original penmanship. It's like the ink exploded all over the document. Thank God I'm typing and not writing. The best thing we could possibly do is to run back into the arms of our Heavenly Father. He hasn't forgotten you. He loves you and is patiently waiting for those who are lost to come back home. Regardless of how He designed us to be, we are all equal in the Eyes of God. We are all created to bring Glory to God. There are many people that have found hope, truth, and peace. They are choosing to turn their lives around by making a stand. A stand along the lines of no longer will they live in a pit of depression. No longer will they feel sorry for themselves. It's awesome to see God move in so many lives. Regardless of who you are, God has a perfect plan for everyone. Fact is, are we willing to lay down our lives? All that we are, all that we have... All for Him, for His Glory. Are we truly opening up our hearts, allowing Him to enter?

God desires for us to be completely surrendered. If we choose not to, it's like giving Picasso a canvas without a brush to paint with, yet the results would never be the same. When we surrender, God opens our eyes and equips us with the right tools to complete His Perfect Will. However, even though this doesn't happen overnight, the results are quite the masterpiece! Talk about "How Great Thou Art". Our God is the Creator of the entire Universe. It's amazing how each and every one of us are designed and placed in the world that we live in. Just pause for a moment and look around you. What do you see? Depending on where you are at, many things could come to mind. Hopefully you're not reading while you're driving. I would hate for you to get pulled over, possibly getting a DWR. But seriously, go outside and take a look around! Hopefully you don't see trash in the street, the smell of musky gas, rusted old beaters parked on blocks and buildings falling apart. I can assure you God didn't create that. Look up though, He literally painted the sky! He allows the sun to set and rise. There are so many colors and there is always something new to see. Talking about paint... I've read testimonies of those who learned to paint with their mouths and even blind men that produced astonishing collections. Incredible!

Have you ever wanted to paint, but feel you might not be any good at it? I suppose some of us have a fear in doing something that has yet to be done. We choose not to step outside of ourselves from what we know. We think we can't do it and the results will just turn out lousy. I remember when God called me to paint. At the time, I haven't drawn anything for about 3 months. I was so used to creating black and white drawings in ink. It's all I knew. The first abstract design that was created was for sure remembered by a lot of people. So famous in fact, they just used one word to describe the drawing. "Banana"! That's right a banana! However, this typical banana was not yellow. In fact, it wasn't typical at all. It's just what most people saw from one quick flash of the drawing. Almost as if the image was just popping out at them. It's a banana, look at me! Hopefully don't eat me, because there wouldn't be anything left of the design. I'd have to say, just like a monkey, I went "bananas" over the drawing. Speaking of bananas, I actually asked a cashier if I could weigh a banana without the peel. I didn't want to pay for something I wasn't going to eat. Anyways, back to the drawing... I have to admit some liked it, some didn't. No matter what we do in life. No matter what is produced, there always happens to be some type of critic out there. Regardless, it's up to us to choose. We can either choose to quit because of criticism, enhance our work, or just let it stay the same. I chose, at that moment, to use that criticism as a form of construction. I continued to practice and re-design the art of abstract. Even though some ideas that were produced were not that great, I continued to advance and move forward.

I didn't want to waste the talent in which God blessed me with, so I cried out to Him. I heard God say, "Go get some paint and a canvas". WHAT!? You want me to do... WHAT!? Are you serious!? I literally asked Him again. Again, I heard Him say, "Go get some paint and a canvas". I had no experience with painting whatsoever. Of course my flesh wanted to rise up and fight. I started to believe that it would be a waste of time and money. Questions even started forming in my mind. What if I might not like the results? Is it even worth it? I can firmly tell you today that it was worth it. It was worth every minute. It was worth every cent. Instead of fighting or pushing it off, I chose to go. The fight was won and the battle was over. I knew that God was calling me to do something great and I chose to say, "Yes Lord, whatever". It's great to have a heart willing to go after God, producing whatever He wants. We need to be bold and know in our hearts that His WILL is what matters most. We have to be willing to say, "Yes" regardless of what He is calling us to do. The results were truly amazing... So amazing in fact they were priceless. Deep in my heart I knew that the first painting should never be sold. The results are way better than what we could ever possibly come up with on our own. Isn't it time to stop living in fear? God equips us with power, love, and self-discipline. Why not try something new? I challenge you to go out, buy some paint and a canvas. Slap a bunch of paint here and there! See what just might turn out!

Ok, so maybe "art" isn't your thing... You might not see it yet, but "art" is truly everywhere. It's the music we listen too, the clothes we wear, the carpet we step on down to the car that we drive. It's the pictures we take, the things we design, the dance moves we make down to what's on this next line. Introducing the new edible pillow! That's right! You not only get a good night's sleep, but when you're craving for that late night's snack, you don't have to go anywhere! Mmmm Pillow... Act now and we'll throw in some edible sheets too! It's all that and so much more! There is always room for comedy anywhere. Why so serious? So regardless of slapping some paint on a "canvas" why not spice up a gift you do have? And no, I'm not talking about placing paint on some carpet either. Or am I? That would be different. I can see it now... Somebody that is just all out, going at it with craziness. What are you doing!!! (Paint is flying everywhere... on the walls, on the ceiling... just everywhere) I'm putting some paint on the carpet! Do you mind!!! Reality check! I'm talking about really using your imagination to come up with something new and improved. Try something different regardless if it's a bit rusty at first. The beauty about being abstract is that everyone doesn't see exactly the same thing. You can use this for so many forms of art other than just paint and ink. Let's take music for example...

Music is awe-inspiring! It's one thing that nobody can take away from you. It's safe and sound, locked in your mind just waiting to breakout into someone else's. However, is it really safe? Most of the time, all you need is some type of catchy beat and you've lured in thousands. It's like the Pied Piper that lured rats with the sound of his pipe. Rats that fell for the trap, just trying to get a piece of some cheese... Awww Rats! Many are sucked in just by the sound. But what about the lyrics? Music, believe it or not, has a major impact on people. What we choose to draw in from the words that we hear effect our lives either in a positive or negative way. I used to listen to music that spoke words of death into my life. There was nothing positive about it. No life was being produced whatsoever. Some artists rap or sing about their possessions, killing people, doing drugs, having sex, making drugs and money. It's what sells. Even though it does sell, we can still choose to flip it and put a positive spin on it. Instead of killing others, we could die to our own flesh. Instead of how much stuff we have, why not give some away or help others gain? Instead of filling ourselves up with garbage, why not bring life to the light? See the brighter side? For example, I should have gotten a DUI today. I was driving under the influence of the Holy Spirit! We could even use this gift as a testimony of God's Love. I am no longer who I used to be. God takes us out from the pit we dug ourselves into and places us in paradise. What we choose to meditate on impacts the path we take. What we draw in eventually reflects who we become. The things we do, the people we hang out all the way down to the conversations spoken, all play vital roles in whom we are developing into.

Musical lyrics that are produced, not only impact the singers, but many people who choose to listen. There are many songs out there with cussing in the lyrics. It's sad that it's putting a negative spin on the younger generation and leading many astray. It's almost like they don't care. Music does impact others whether we pay attention to it or not. Life and death are in the power of the tongue. We can lie to others, but we can't lie to God. He always knows the truth about what's going on in the darkness of night. There will be a day when it's brought to the light. Believe it or not, music artists are role models. I'm sure they have some type of writers block at times. It's likely that you might have lyrics to only half of a song? Possibly even more than one song? Here is something that came to mind, which I don't understand why it's not produced yet. We hold keys to unlocking the future. Fact is we should put our ideas out there. Why not take two songs that are only half completed and mix them? During the half way point you could either speed up or slow down the tempo depending on how the other song is produced. I would make a whole album like that. I know DJ's do this all the time in clubs to tie in songs, but why not have a song that is 2 in 1 already? Music producers could do so much with that and change the music industry! You could even leave clues from one song to advance to another... similar to playing mind games. There are even hidden songs on certain tracks, in which you have to either let the track play or fast forward until you here the lyrics. → Gibberish... Anyway, hear that sound!? With the beats that are pumping, I'm sure there has to be dancers in action.

Dancing is another form of art and I'm not talking about exotic dancing either. It's sad that some choose to sell their bodies for money. Oops, I talked about it. If they only knew deep down inside who they truly are meant to be... I'm sure they have so much more potential other than that. This type of dancing alone is so seductive. It draws the attention aside, leaving you vulnerable. It tends to lead others astray so that their focus is locked in. It catches us to a point where at times we choose not to let go, somewhat similar to booby-traps. Anyway, scratch that. Let's get back to some real dancing... I think it's amazing how people out there can break dance. They literally break the meaning of dance. The moves that some clicks do are very impressive. Truly off the chain. Why is it usually off the "chain" anyway? I mean, this book isn't chained up and many dancers aren't shackled down in chains breaking out moves. Or are they? For now, I'll just switch it up a bit and say it's off the page! I'd encourage anyone that loves to dance to never give up! Imagine something different and place it in action regardless of how long it takes to master it. There are so many different things you could do on the dance floor. Especially a lot of invisible gestures to place into reality. This goes far beyond "mimes" too. Have the mindset to never stop using your imagination. For now, I'd like to talk about the Bernie Dance.

Have you ever had the urge to go out on the dance floor and do the Bernie? I actually did this at a wedding. I can see it now. Look Honey Bear, there's us getting married, there's the bridal bouquet toss, and there is... What The!? Some might wonder what that is!? Well... I can tell you. Have you ever watched the movie entitled, "Weekend at Bernie's"? To do the dance, simply bend you head back like your having a nose bleed and go all out. Put your back into it and give your whole body a shake. Shake like your twitching from an electric shock. You might even want to check it out on YouTube. Bernie Dance Craze. Some other dance moves came to my attention. Why not stumble out onto the dance floor acting like your all drunk, but it's just a gimmick. You then take off your shoe and make it rain with paper punches, evidently called Chad. Hold up!? Wouldn't that be snow? Regardless, it would be off the page! It possibly might be this page, because I've never seen it done. Who knows, maybe it has been done and the manager got upset. No problem, we'll just clean up the mess. During the clean up, we found a <u>*couple dollars in*</u>

change. We'll save this for later. Why don't we bust a move to another form of art…?

How about Interior Design? Isn't it breathtaking!? Quick! Someone call a doctor, I can't breathe! But seriously… it's the design surroundings we choose to live in. I should say choose to live around, because it'd be crazy to actually live inside a design. Yet we are designed by God, so we are living in a design… His Design. Let's get back to the rooms. It's almost as if you could have different mood swings as you walk from one room of your house to another. I always thought about hanging up a surfboard on a wall that looks as if a shark has sunken his teeth in it, just ripping it apart. You then could have somewhat of a sandy beach section actually on the floor along with some type of waterfall for a wall. There is so much you could do for design. I also thought about having some type of room where everything is like all lopsided, yet still balanced to a point where it could work. It would be different to own a bench that split apart at the end forming into part of the wall. Also, I'm sure you could even have items bolted upside down, hanging from the ceiling. Ok, so maybe this is a bit too abstract? I have to say, remodeling rooms to a house is amazing too. I think it's cool to place any open cabinets actually into a wall. This saves on lots of space to where the cupboard actually looks flush with the wall, yet when you open it… BAM! Storage space! Besides all the nick-knack stuff and pictures on the wall, what about the exterior side of the building too?

There is so much you can do with outside of the homes we live. It's really neat to see before and after pictures of what people have done. I love the brick pieces that are used to either go around support beams or used for the new siding. Adding some type of veranda to the building is amazing as well. There are ideas for new driveways, down to pathways leading out back to landscaping. People have added swimming pools or ponds with small waterfalls built in. On one hand, others have taken out unnecessary trees or shrubs for a better view. On the other hand, some have placed new plants or bushes for an observation that's noteworthy. Taking notes? At times, we would never know that places acquired a new look by the development of remodeling. Even the resale value increases! Is it time that your home could use an upgrade? Anyways, I could go on and on about this and that or whatever. Yet if we are serious, why not give it a shot and make something new? I mean, it is the quarters you live in. And, no... I'm not talking about the change we picked up off that dance floor, at least not yet. Even if you live in an apartment complex, it wouldn't hurt to at least make some type of suggestion to the owners. There is always improvement for new kitchen appliances. Out with the old, in with the new. Speaking of kitchens, want to get something to eat?

Cooking is an extraordinary form of art! It's truly more than just following a bunch of recipes and directions off of some piece of paper. There is a gift and talent in cooking. Not everyone can do this. I remember trying to cook a steak inside using an iron skillet. I don't want to get into a whole lot of details here, but let's just say this... Bottom line; just make sure you put the steak on first, then the oil. I'm not talking about motor oil either. Even the chicken turned out dry in the oven. Though, that's not as bad as burning popcorn in the microwave. Ain't nobody got time for that! Ah, the wonderful microwave. It's the type of generation we live in. We want things now, right away. Even for that fact, we want it so fast that even the microwave is too slow. I highly admire chiefs and their skills. I mean, we all have to eat and it's much better to have some type of home cooked meal than nuked stew. When food is slowly cooked, it just tastes better. I love to eat. Did I mention that I love to eat? Hold up, I'll be back in like 10 to 15 minutes. I could just type a bunch of .... or ______ _____ __ but how long is 15 minutes to the reader? I mean we all read at a different pace and most would just overlook all the dots or lines anyway. It wouldn't mean a thing to some. Ok, so I'm back... I had to go get some popcorn and some other snacks. Mmm MMmm! Food! Such a form of art!

So, Art... It's truly all around us. Things that we smell, touch, taste, hear, and see. Five beautiful senses in which God designed. How Great Thou Art! I'm telling you, there is no limit to how much God has in store for us! Never place a limit on what He can do in and through us. We, ourselves, are the only ones that place limits on what God can do. Be optimistic! Be inspired! Have an open heart and be willing to receive. Be willing to try something new and improved! Use your imagination in which God has blessed us with. Use it to bring Glory to God! Ask yourself, "Am I using the gifts and talents that God blessed me with in a positive way? Will we choose to waste it, allowing it to form into garbage? If so, that's truly sad. Be encouraged! Don't waste the gifts and talents in your life, allowing them to transform into trash. There is an old saying – One man's trash becomes another man's treasure. I truly believe God will strip those of shattered gifts and bless the ones that are willing to say, "Yes!" I'll go! I'll do whatever it takes! I also believe God can repair and restore the gifts that were lost. At any rate, True Treasure's in Heaven.

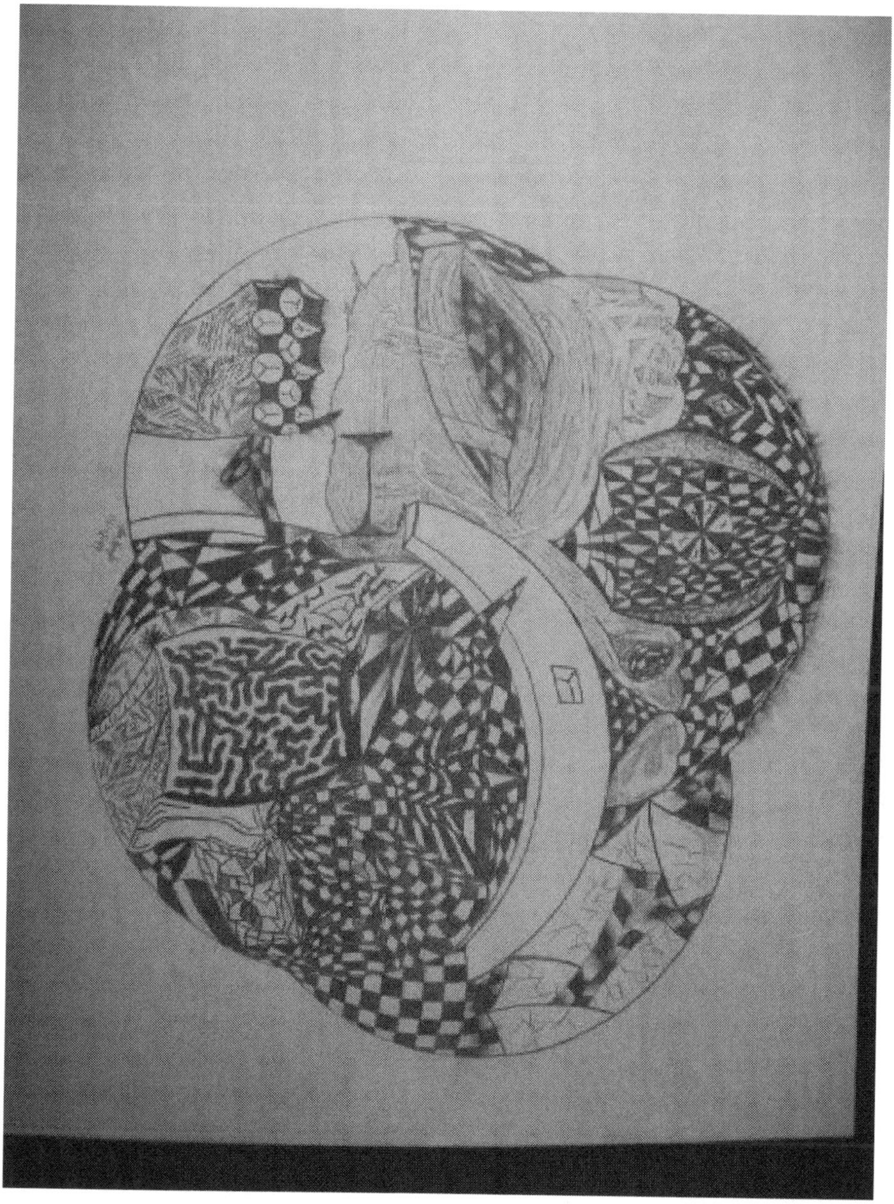

“Banana” By: Jon Koegle … 1st abstract drawing

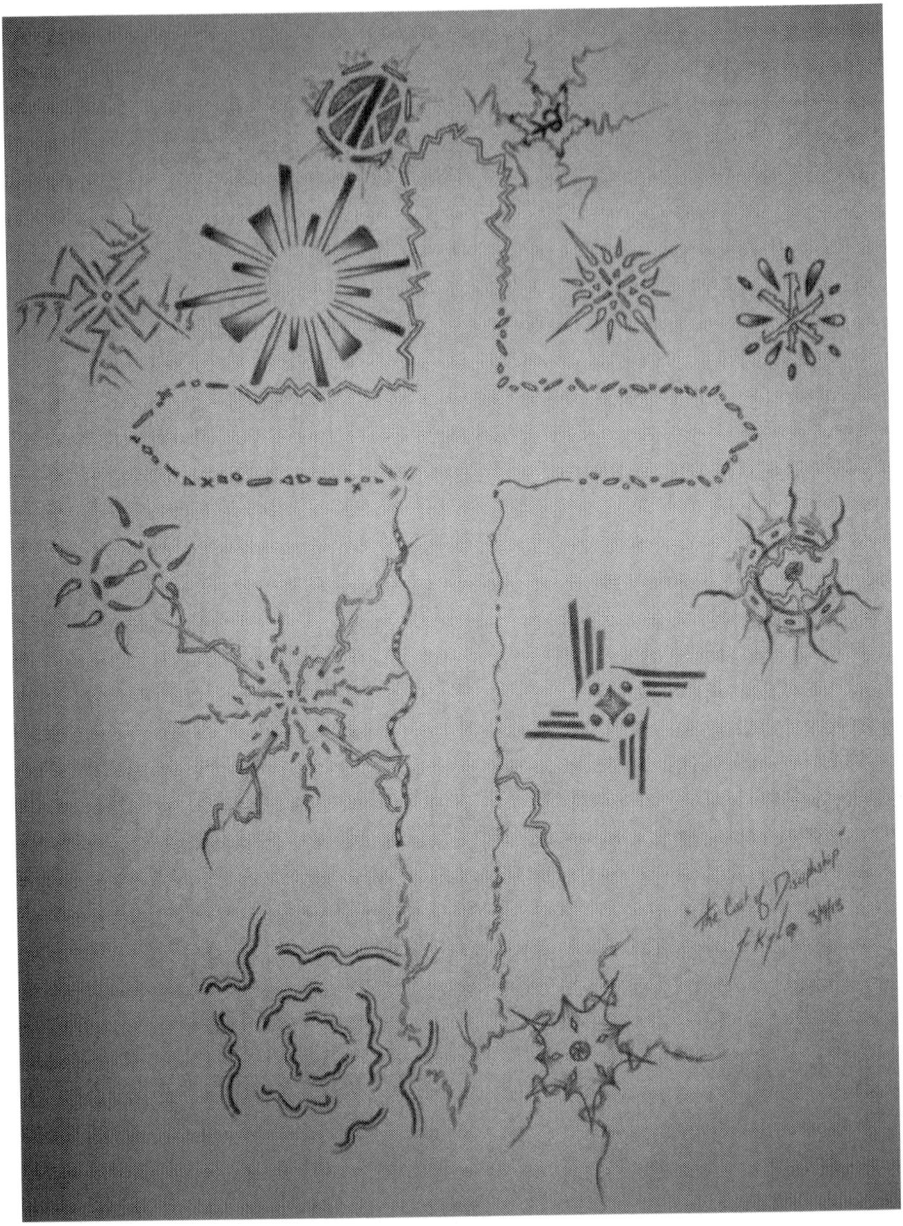

"The Cost of Discipleship" By: Jon Koegle ... Years later, now living for God and using His gift of art for His Glory.

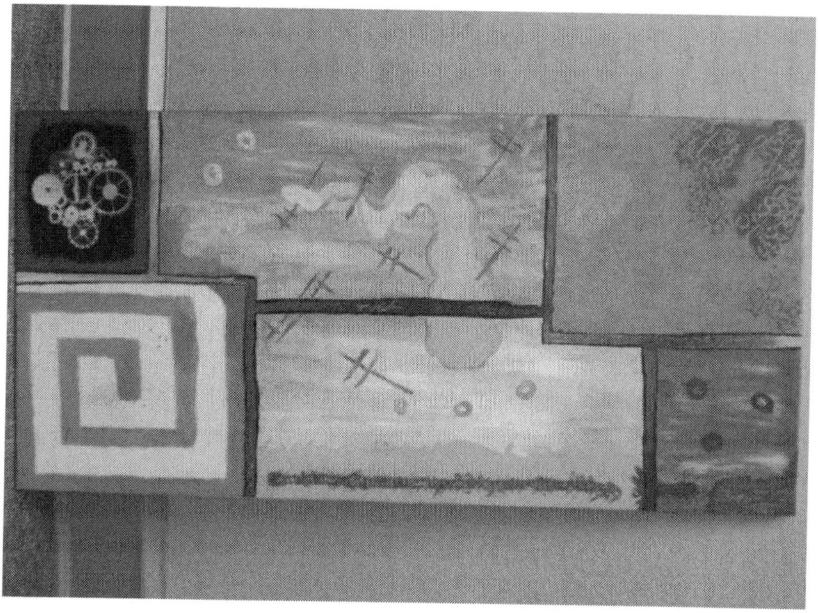

"Sky District" By: Jon Koegle ... Possibly my 5th painting, 7/4/13

"Come As You Are" By: Jon Koegle ... Ideas placed into action for a brother. We don't need to wait to come to God. He will accept us as we are.

Chapter 01

Perceptions of Deception

Well, you've finally made it to chapter 01 and the book hasn't blown up. No explosion, no Kaboom, nothing. Even though this book hasn't blown to pieces, I'm sure it has "blown up" in many other ways. I'm sure some type of spark ignited a firework and blown some imaginative ideas into play. Can fireworks actually produce ideas? Is it possible for ideas to actually play with each other? Anyways, fireworks can be deceiving at times. It's happened many of times. You light the fuse, stand back and wait for the right moment. As you are waiting looking up into the sky, a plane flies by with a banner. That's odd... The banner reads, "Will you marry me?" Now at this point, the fireworks are supposed to be going off. You begin to realize they're not. If this were a real story, I'm sure the woman wouldn't mind, especially if her heart was saying yes. Just in case you are wondering... Yes, hearts can speak and "fireworks" would already being going off in her mind. Later, you begin to walk up to the fireworks. At the time, it seems as if they really are duds. Once you get really close, they begin to go off and you start to take cover. As you are sprinting away, you end up tripping, planting your face in the ground. Now that's a Kodak moment! Hey, it could happen. We all have our "moments" in life. Just like a firework that is delayed, we come across situations that can deceive us. After giving in, some tend to "blow up" in our face... others are just plain mind games.

I mean, that's where the battle begins in the first place. It all starts in our mind. As we set out and depart into the world, we make choices on a daily basis. These choices usually form in our minds before making a decision. There are many choices in life, just don't let those choices choose you. We decide. Our minds do not control us, we control our minds. At times, it's like we are zombies. BRAIN!!! Many of us have been there. We wake up, possibly not wanting to get out of bed. Then once we finally do, we rely on some coffee or an energy drink to help wake us up and get ready for the day. Can you smell it? MMmm! That sweet aroma! I wonder how much money people would actually save if they put down the "drinks". Let's take a moment to think about this. On average, let's just say some wake up juice cost about $2 per day. So, on average this comes down to roughly $800 in a full year. This does include tax. Now some even choose to drink even more than one per day. Pretty crazy huh? What's even crazier is how we choose to let it control us. Ok, so maybe it's not coffee or an energy drink for you. But, it might be an expensive cell phone or what about cable. I guarantee that some would be very upset if they didn't have this throughout the day. I'm sure we would wake up just fine knowing that this money could have gone towards something else. Towards something at least more enjoyable. Something that will last, lasting longer than a few measly hours. Are you curious to what else this could have gone to? Would you spend it all in one place? What would you choose to buy? What about going on vacation? How about a big screen TV? Or how about ________________! Imagine that! Imagine what?

What was I talking about again? I could just read the last paragraph over again, but that would be too easy. Oh, yah! I was talking about "Waking Up!" We go throughout the day and something important comes across our way. Then, not even realizing it, BAM! We forget and the message is twisted in our minds. I don't believe the message is completely lost. It just takes some time to find it. It just takes some time to sort things out. It's kind of similar to seeking the mysteries of life like poet. You need some keys to decode it. 7H15 M3554G3 53RV35 7O PROV3 HOW OUR M1ND5 C4N DO 4M4Z1NG 7H1NG5! 1MPR3551V3 7H1NG3! 1N 7H3 B3G1NN1NG 17

M1GH7 H4V3 B33N H4RD, BU7 YOUR M1ND 1S R34D1NG 17 4U70M471C4LLY W17H0U7 3V3N 7H1NK1NG 4B0U7 17! PR377Y COOL HUH? 1 5UPP053 ONLY C3R741N P30PL3 C4N R34D 7H15. C4N U R34D 7HI5? 17 15 P0551BL3! JU57 B3 7H4NKFUL 7H47 7H3 3N71R3 BOOK 15N'7 L1K3 7H15. FOR ON3, 17 WOULD 74K3 M3 FOR3V3R 70 7YP3 7H15. FOR 7WO, 1'M 5UR3 YOU WOULDN'7 3NJOY 17. Anyways, let's get back to regular English. Let's get back to the point.

At this point you might be wondering, "Where is Chapter 02?" Some of you might have noticed right away that Chapter 02 is missing. If not, you do now since you have read the last sentence. Is it possible that someone tore some pages out before you purchased the book? I must say, "It had to be a steal of a deal!" It's ok, don't be alarmed. Don't put the book down or run back to the bookstore trying to get your money back. Well, I can't force you. Depending on how far it is could you actually run that far? I wonder if they would actually give you your money back? MMMmm... Now that's worth a shot. Wait, what are we shooting? That's right; we are shooting the words right off this page. Don't be deceived. By all means, this is not my intention. Put the gun down. Some of you might have gone back to Chapter 03 just to make sure it was what you read. I hope you don't tend to call, write, or ask why; possibly even saying some inappropriate things. I might just hang up on you. *CLICK* If I chose to do that, the book would have ended already. I'm sure there would be a lot of heated people out there. I can see it now, riots being started while blowing hot air. Why the phrase, "blowing hot air" anyway? It's not like we are filling up a balloon and drifting somewhere. Or are we? Are we in Oz? All in all, yes. Not in Oz, but I meant to take out the 2nd chapter. Wait... wouldn't that be chapter 06? Well, you know what I mean... and if you know what I mean, are you reading my mind? Yes, in a way you are reading my mind since this came out of my mind. You might ask, "Why did you take out

Chapter 02?" If that were the case, I would be reading your mind. If you really want to know, I have my reasons.

I wouldn't be surprised if a lady was reading this that had a dog named "Toto". However, I might be a little surprised if that lady's name was also "Dorothy". Then I would have to wonder if I was actually in Oz. If you've seen the movie, you know the wizard used an idea that was full of deception. Anyways, back to the reasons. Honestly, I just wanted something different to be published. After all, I am the author. This book is the real deal. Some might see the miss spelled words or miss used grammar as I type, yet it's the real me. This is how I am designed to be. I have to say, English was by far my worst subject. As long as you know or at least understand what I'm saying, it makes sense... right? If I allowed an editor to take out some parts or change several things, then it wouldn't be fully me. It would be left. There would be missing ingredients and the formula would have been tampered with. I would like to encourage all of you to be yourself in who you are designed to be. Don't get me wrong, it's good to seek advice on a lot of stuff; however it's up to us to either accept it by following through with it or just plain reject it by tossing it out the window. Hopefully this book wouldn't be found in the street by someone tossing it out their window. However, I'm sure someone else would come along noticing it lying in the street. They would possibly pick it up, be inspired and even start to produce a change in their lives.

It's up to us to change, not being forced by someone else. I know I'm taking a huge risk in putting a book like this out on the market. Yet, I know it's what God wants. I personally have never read a book with a chapter missing out from it, unless someone actually ripped out some pages. If some pages were actually torn out, I'm sure you would know. Maybe you wouldn't? I do know, however, you would notice some type of gap in the glue. Now that would be a genius idea! Actually having a gap would give it even more of a visual effect to go along with the missing chapter. I would then have to wonder if people would actually buy it. I wonder if book stores would actually hold something like that in their store for sale. I'm sure they would get many responses. "Did you know there are some pages missing from this book?" Yup, that's how the author created it. They do similar things like this in movies, so why not do it in books? It just might put the readers on the edge of their seat. Maybe you're not on the edge yet. How about now? Are you on the edge of your seat? I challenge you to live life to the full extent. Live your life on the edge. I don't mean doing dumb things that will get you into trouble either. What I mean is to really live. Place your ideas into action. I'm sure you have a reasonable imagination.

Another reason why I decided to take out Chapter 02 is just because of the simple fact that I wanted to mess with your mind. I hope your mind doesn't mind. Do you mind? I'm sure it doesn't mind because you are choosing to read on. Hopefully you aren't misled by this chapter either. Several are deceived and lead astray in this world. At times, many choose to dwell on the things they can't change. When this happens, life still goes on around you. Choose to focus on the things you can change. I believe many of us hold keys to unlock thoughts that are trapped. Break free from the trap. Quit getting lured and sucked in to doing things your heart doesn't desire. Quit trying to be something you're not, just so you can get noticed or become popular. I challenge you to take a risk and use the time that we are blessed with wisely. Place something different out in this world. Something that you've longed to produce, yet never did. Maybe you didn't have the resources? I urge you to ask around and get some support! Maybe you stopped because of what others thought? I remember reading something awhile back that stated the first automobile was slower than horses. Now look at them! Vehicles would leave them in the dust! Yay or Nay? Be encouraged to get back on track, even if this takes stepping out from ourselves. Choose to take a step outside your comfort zones. I can tell you, I was not comfortable at first in typing this book. Nor was I comfortable when I first started painting, yet the results are truly amazing.

I challenge you to start seeing things in life differently. It's a great idea to carry around some type of notepad or device. This way when important ideas and things come to mind, we can jot them down and remember them. We need to learn to lay down that pride. Learn to wake up and smell the bacon! Why does the word need to be coffee all the time in that phrase? Let's switch it up a bit shall we? Some of us think we'll remember, yet don't. Not even five minutes go by and we are so bombarded with other things we sometimes forget important information. We might be sitting in an office just staring at the computer. We wonder, "Now what was I was going to do?" Then we remember that the bacon is on the stove. We only remember because the fire alarm goes off, annoying the life right out of us. Speaking of writing things down, I wrote this down the other day. Computerized Wallpaper. How awesome would it be to change the outlook of your walls in your room with just a click of a button? This is creativity that is programmable! One minute you could be on the moon, out in space... The next hour or so, you could be in the Amazon jungle! There would be no end to this genius idea! Are you curious?

I'm no computer whiz, but that idea should be possible. It's the process of making the virtual become reality. I have to admit that some are plugged so far into the virtual world; to them that is actually reality. Curiosity... I'm feeling a little froggy, time to take a leap. Leap right into the unknown, because the left is already known. Why is it "froggy" most of the time anyway? Why not using a different phrase? Ever had the urge to bark? It's the dog in me wanting to come out. Some of us talk a big game, yet when it comes down to play... it's all bark and no bite, just chilling on the side lines. Again, I challenge you to take a risk making the unknown become known. However, when we choose to place this into action, hopefully we have some type of sense. It's wise to use some type of form in relation to good judgment. We should know a difference between what's right and what's wrong. What we choose to decide plays a critical role on how our day carries out. Seriously, would we set our life on a roll of some dice? Come on... lucky number!!! Seven! Ah... Crap! Yet some choose to still gamble their life away. How about cards? Poker? Blackjack? They choose to risk it all to try and get rich quick. There is way more to life than money. It takes a lot of time to earn money. Many hours put into thinking of ideas and actually placing them into action. Time is spent on many, many situations and things. However, I've come to find out that time is invested when it's spent on people. Why? Why don't we let the magic 8 ball decide for us? Yes, now that's a splendid idea!

Let's see, where did I put that thing..? Oh yea, here it is. I placed it behind a box of reasons why. There are so many questions to where we want to know the answers too. Why this and why that? Well, if life was an algebra problem I'm sure most wouldn't want to solve the answer to why (y). Why not ask the magic eight ball a few questions shall we? Like as if we are going to get some genius response from an eight ball? If we took it apart, do you believe that there would be some nickel sized men giving you an appropriate response? Now what should we ask? Oh, I know. Why not start with that first question from the last paragraph? "How come time is invested when it's spent on people?" *SHAKE* *SHAKE* *SHAKE* Oh, Look here comes the response! "Don't ask me I'm a ball." How genius! That makes a lot of sense to me. But really, I truly believe time is invested because you're actually with the person. You want to see them succeed in life. You're spending time getting to know one another and building a relationship! It's important to develop a strong connected relationship. We have a better "feel" for others and what's going on inside them. It's crazy on how many hours go throughout the day where we choose to sit in front of our televisions or mess around on our phones. We live in an age where there is hardly any communication anymore. People text and send out e-mails rather than talk on the phone. What's even crazier is that our language is getting distorted. Many choose to use sentences with words that are just one letter or a number to make a full word. For instance some actually type the word HAND to mean have a nice day.

IDK bout u, bt dats %-). It myt B fstr, yet f we contu2 dev a habit N2 doiN dis, we eventually *t ritN thus as wel. Onestly, sum myt B so %-) RN it's takN em 4ever 2 read dis 2 undrst& w@ I'm tlkN bout. Sum myt have np readN dis. Let's get back to normal plain English shall we? Honestly, that even took me longer to type than what I'm typing right now. LOL. I actually wonder if people are laughing out loud when they type LOL. Let's ask the magic eight ball! "Are people actually laughing as they type LOL?" *SHAKE* *SHAKE* *SHAKE* And the response is: "Don't count on it." I believe this is an appropriate answer. Some might be laughing in their minds, but are they actually laughing out loud. And if so, how loud? Loud enough to where the neighbor a few doors down is disturbed? Now that would be pretty loud. At times I'm sure a lot of us say things without thinking about it, then realize later we shouldn't have followed through with it. At least on facebook there is a delete button, but what about real life. What about the connection? No, I'm not talking about the internet either. I'm talking about caring for others feeling and emotions. If we have conflicts with one another we can choose to make things right again in person. I challenge you to ask for forgiveness toward some people you have offended. Also, even if others have offended you choose to forgive them. Quit holding onto that bitterness or resentment. We even use the offenses to strike back at others whom have done nothing wrong at the moment. We vent in the wrong places at the wrong people. If we hold onto it for so long, it will eat us alive. It will devour us producing death.

What about death? "What is the meaning of life?" *SHAKE* *SHAKE* *SHAKE* --- "Focus and Ask Again." What? *SHAKE* *SHAKE* *SH-*... Ooops! *SLAM* *BREAK* *CRACK* *SPLIT* Ahhh, Man! Now I'll never know! Well, at least I know there wasn't any nickel sized men in there, just a bunch of ooze and responses. So, many ask what is the meaning of life? I'm sure they would get quite a few different responses too. I boldly would like to state that the true meaning of life is found when we pursue Jesus Christ as His disciple. We must choose to be obedient to His commands and walk with Him. We must learn from Him by communication and follow through with His commands in and through action. We must also spend time in His Holy Word and Pray, not for ourselves all the time, but others. We are created for His Glory, to bring Glory unto Him. I encourage you to worship, praise and seek Him daily. Some might say that this is boring, however it is a choice. We will have to answer one day and be held accountable for all that we have done. All I know is that "my way" didn't produce fulfillment. It produced nothing but emptiness!

Think about it. Many look back over the years and wonder why things have fallen apart. They even achieve what they have set out to accomplish, yet still feel so empty inside. Seriously, once we reach the top there is nothing there. We choose to pursue many things, thinking that we will find some sort of meaning behind them. What do we pursue? All sorts of entertainment, sex, success, wealth, even doing good to one another or trying to be nice. People have been in pursuit of all these things and more for years, yet still are filling a void inside. They still feel an emptiness that longs to be filled. Only God can give and produce pure life. Through Christ we will find contentment, joy and satisfaction. Be made known that God loves us so much and desires the best for us. I admit, this might not be the easiest life to some, but I can say it's the most fulfilling. To some the easiest way of life is already being taken on a wide path to destruction. But, what about being rebuilt? What about having that restoration instead of damaging yourself and others that tend to follow you?

Speaking of emptiness, I'm a bit hungry at the moment. Thank God for the *couple dollars in change* that we found on the dance floor. Let's see what that change can produce! What to choose... What to choose? There are so many items to choose from in a vending machine. All of the sudden we are drawn in by a sparkle flash of light. Something catches our eye that we crave for. I'm not sure what kind of snack satisfies your hunger, but I love beef jerky. As the buttons are pressed "B4" you begin to realize another item pops out long side of it. Hmmm.... I wonder what this could be? Who could have possibly placed this there? And Why? Some of you are like, duh? It has to be the vending machine guy, right? Anyways... Reaching into the machine, you pull out the jerky along with *some type of key*. U812 is imprinted on the side. Assuming by the structure and shape of the key it goes to a locker. Possibly a small locker, like those you find at a mall. I speculate, what could be inside? Instead of contemplating about it, we'll save this for later when we arrive at the correct locker. Pretty crazy.

It's crazy, but as soon as we are born we begin to die. We will not live on earth forever and only have a certain amount of time. I urge you to spend your time wisely. Don't you want a life worth living for? Don't you want to see others around you succeed? Wouldn't you like to be a part of their success? When people gather together, a lot more can get accomplished than just having one individual from the start. That's right, we all have to start somewhere but where do we finish? I can assure you eternal life begins after the finish line. Eternal life begins after we die. So why do we live now? All of us walk through many tests and trials. I'd like to encourage you all, learn from your mistakes because we all make them. I'm sure there might be some in theis book, yet that won't stop me from publishing it! Be bold, be real. Be different and take some risks. Don't wrap yourself up around what others think of you. Don't allow others to tell you that you cannot become something. We all become something. We all are destined for greatness! Take advantages of the opportunities around us and succeed! Strive to become more than what you already know. Make an impact by influencing others and lead them in a positive direction, full of heart and compassion. You might be coming up on the end of this chapter, yet I can almost guarantee you it's not the end of your life. Life does not have a remote. We have to choose to get up and change it!

¡uıƃǝq noʎ ǝɹǝɥʍ sı puǝ ǝɥʇ ~ Remember when I challenged you to start seeing things differently? Sometimes when people are fighting colds they use the phrase, I'm feeling a little "under the weather." How can you be "under" the weather anyway? We already are, but caught in it. To get well, most stack up on medication hoping to get "over" the weather. Once well, they see the sunny side of day. Things are brighter and much clearer. To most people they would probably think this is the end of the book since we started at Chapter 07 and worked our way back to Chapter 01. However, I'd like to make things a little more clearly for you. If you read "Chapter 01" backwards, you discover that the 10th Chapter is formed. On to Chapter 10 shall we!?

Chapter 10

Mirror

As you look at yourself in a mirror, what do you see? This goes far beyond the pimples that some choose to pop or even the buggers we get out from our nose. I'm sure if you noticed some buggers, you just wouldn't walk away from the mirror without doing something about it. Would you? I can see it now. As I'm having a conversation, just noticing something that consistently catches your eye. Do we at least have the decency to address others in regards to what they might not know? This can go far beyond the brownie smears on a face. This can even relate to the way people choose to behave. Thousands look at themselves in the mirror every day, yet some are not happy with themselves. Why? I mean, we have to live with ourselves for the rest of our lives... So why not do something about it if you are not happy with who you are? I'm not talking about plastic surgery either. I'm talking about building up your confidence, truly being who you are designed to be. Not having a fear to put your ideas and talents into action, regardless if others might not like it. Actually willing to step up and risk it all to place something new out on the market. Many of us are destined to help change this world for the better, yet time after time we choose not to.

We rather choose to hide behind masks and imitate others. We rather choose to put on shows and be fake, letting our real self evaporate into the darkness. We "act" certain ways before certain people, yet once we are behind them the real "act" begins. And why? What for? Just so we can be popular? Just so we can be accepted? Just so we can gain fame or even to be noticed? Many sob behind closed doors wondering what is happening to their lives and where they are going. Many are scared to be their real "selves". You might ask, "How do you know this?" I know this because in a way, this used to be me. I want to encourage all of you to be yourself, becoming who you are destined and designed to be. Be yourself, because when you do that's when you will actually become noticed. You'll stand out and be different from the "ways" of the world. You'll be bold enough to make a stand, going in the right direction and succeeding in life. You'll be brave enough to be committed to your destiny, allowing nothing to stand in your way. You'll be courageous! And so what if some don't like what they see? Even though there are many critics out there, are you willing to let them get the best of you? So, as you look into a mirror what do you see?

We wake up every day and look at ourselves in the mirror. Some not only look at themselves in the mirror, they actually become the mirror image. Do you see yourself becoming the next superstar? Do you "mirror" after your favorite actor or role model? If so, still choose to be yourself. Don't choose to be the next somebody that's already popular. Choose to be the next unknown to become known! Be the next nobody to become somebody. Time and time again, I tell others, "All Glory to God." I wouldn't be who I am today if I didn't choose to surrender my life and become whom God destined me to be. It's a choice we choose to take. We choose to follow through and commit ourselves, being in line with His perfect will. I want to be so far gone in Christ, so that when others look at me, they see Jesus in me. Every day we have an opportunity to get ready. We face moments that either impact us for the better or for the worse. We make choices and allow ourselves to go there. To go where? Well, where did you get this book for one? For two, you obviously enjoy reading it otherwise you wouldn't be here.

About every morning we make sure we are dressed appropriately for work. A lot of us want the latest fashion and style, spending thousands of dollars on clothing that we don't bother wearing after awhile. Even when we are going out on a date, we tend to really make sure we look good. We put on make-up to look superior or more attractive than what we already are. Maybe I should change "we" to ladies? However, depending on what the "make-up" is for, just about all of us put some on at some point in our lives. A lot of us dress up for Halloween in October. For a moment, we act like something we're not. Many prowl the streets ringing door bells for some goodies. Later on that night, we stuff our faces with gobs of candy and then wonder why stomachaches form overnight. In similarity, we face many situations in our lives that "make-up" us. We are drawn into certain things that catch our eyes. We choose to model or go after stuff that we have a strong desire for. Be advised: Everything that we indulge in makes a vital impact on our image. Choose wisely on what we carry out throughout the days because as we develop, our character is not easy to change.

Think about it, year after year we live our lives doing the same things. Most people go through the same routine every day, every week. Regardless of what schedule is placed into practice, it reflects an impact on our image. Habits are formed, reflecting our character. We go through trials and testing to gain experience that puts either a positive or negative spin on our lives. In order to correct some negative spins, we must go through situations to place positive things into practice. Opportunities are around us daily to place this practice into action. A magical little fairy isn't going to pop up out of nowhere and sprinkle some dust on you, creating an instant change. *BAM* Your changed instantly! No, this takes time. This takes patience. We must be willing to follow through with some type of commitment and self-discipline. I'm sure you have developed some type of ideas to place into action just from reading this book.

However, we must choose to follow through with it. Have some motivation and make some commitment into following through with change.

Self-discipline is huge! If we lack discipline in our own lives, we will lose control of what matters most and practically do whatever we want. We allow our minds to control us and go after anything and everything our flesh desires. Time and time again, people chose to place "play" before work when you can simply just play at work or during work. I'm not talking about doing nothing either and just slacking off. I'm talking about actually having fun at your job and placing what matters most first. I'm talking about actually being a reliable asset to the company and organization. I'm talking about changing your life and having fun doing it. We should have a mindset to get the high priority stuff done first in our lives and then go from there. We shouldn't allow the needs of others to dictate our schedule either. There has to come a time where "no" is an acceptable answer to allow more important things to get taken care of first. Instead of saying no, important tasks accumulate and pile up, making it a bit more complicated to eventually succeed. It's like garbage overflowing from the trash can. I've seen trash just pile up, over and over on top of more junk. Most of the time, people refuse to even take the trash out. It's pretty easy to take the garbage out; it's just a matter of actually doing it. The same goes for our lives. Take the trash out from our lives that have accumulated over the years!

If I chose to eat practically whatever I want, whenever I want and did nothing about it. I would eventually become a fat tub of lard. Really!? Well, not literally. Can I get some butter with that please!? I know, because I've done it and lived it. I have gone from weighing about 140 lbs. to roughly 200 lbs. in a matter of 10 months. At the time, I chose to do nothing about it. I did notice that I was getting a belly on me and decided that enough was enough. I need some "self-discipline" in my life to get moving. Those pounds are not just going to fade away. It takes time and effort. I can literally say that the work out routines sucked. I actually had to fight against my flesh and discipline myself weekly to see the results take place. After about 3 months of consistent sweat and fat fighting effort, I began to look better and feel healthier. This goes far beyond just losing weight too. If we know we are behind with work, why do we choose to have fun and act like it's just going to get done on its own? If we want to get better at a certain activity or sport, why do we choose not to practice or even play harder? We choose to do other things that are not important and waste opportunities for success. We fill ourselves up with so called happiness that doesn't last. When we are bummed out we even take further steps into anything entertaining just so we can "feel" happy again. It's time we stopped being scared to do important things or place new ideas into action. It's time we did things that truly do matter. It's time we took a stand and fight for what's right. Fight for your life!

I mean, it's your life. You have to live with "yourself" for the rest of your life. So why not make the best of it? All of us have 24 hours in a day. We decide, we choose on how we spend the time. It's time we stopped feeling sorry for ourselves. Time and time again, people feel pitiful, digging themselves deeper into a pit of misery and hopelessness. They feel depressed, disappointed and let down. Why are there so many critics out there? Why are there so many haters? There are tons of people that make fun of others and let others down. Why? I believe that those who do have some type of jealously or bitterness built up inside them. They put others down just so they can feel good about themselves or attract attention. If so, why not collaborate to gain something from the situation? Why not take a risk, coming up with ideas to expand or influence others for the better? For instance: If others make fun of a new song produced that reaches a lot of people, why not they, themselves try to come up with something better? Why not possibly give some advice or input in an encouraging, positive way? Choose to turn negative situations into positive ones. Take a risk and draw that line!

I'm sure most could agree that as we look at ourselves in a mirror we see an image of ourselves. Wouldn't it be weird if it was someone else? I'm sure most of us would be freaked out. They do some type of special effects like this in the movies, but this is real life. However, some people actually do see someone else. They don't see themselves as they see their reflection. They don't see themselves as they truly are meant to be. Regardless of who you are, we all are created for a special purpose. Be encouraged to reach out and help others. Be encouraged to even seek the help needed from others! Find your destiny and impact this world for the better. Our mirror image is pretty much like a reverse representation of us. Think about, or why not give it a try. Go, get up out of your seat and find a mirror. Are you there? If not, whatever... As you raise your left hand, your right hand is raised in the mirror. I believe this is pretty trippy. So what we are looking at is basically an opposite perspective. At times, we should look at our lives and the way we live in a different way. We should look at some things from a different perspective. We should have a different point of view such as a mirror image.

Now, if I chose to write this chapter all backwards in a mirror imagine I don't believe most would take the time to actually find a mirror and read the entire chapter. This would attract some attention though if you were reading this book on the go. Imagine walking into a restroom finding a person reading this book, which the book is right next to a mirror. What about seeing a person using a hand held mirror to read this book? The person would have to be fairly close to the mirror to even read the words to create sentences, but not only that fact to actually make out the context. I just so happen to type at least one paragraph as in a mirror form. So, you might want to grab a mirror or go to a mirror. If not, I suppose you could just skip over an entire paragraph. It's up to you. In regards to that, I can see it now... "What the!?" What are you doing? What are you reading? This could possibly even get others attention into asking, "Where did you possibly get that book?" Where can I get one? Then you can meet someone new and have a conversation with a stranger you don't even know.

Do you have a mirror yet? I have to admit, when looking at some mirrors there happens to be a lot of junk on them. Have you ever tried looking out a window, trying to see past the gunk? It is quite possible; however the view or picture we see is not fully intact. We can't see the full image, only parts. We then use our imagination to create the rest of the image to make whole. The longer the junk sits, the harder it is to have a clean clear image. The same goes with our lives. The longer we choose to let negative situations sit and simmer, the more it builds into our lives. It adapts to us, making us who we are because we choose to believe it. Believe truth and become clean! If we spent some time cleaning the junk away from our view, it's much easier to see and make out. The same goes with our own lives. Honestly, if we choose to do a half fast job, then all the junk just turns into smears which distorts the picture entirely. Yet if we spend some time in making sure all the junk is out of the way and off the glass, our view or perspective becomes much clearer. It takes time to do jobs correctly. It takes time to change our lives. If changed just happened overnight, we wouldn't learn anything and no experience would be gained. Our character wouldn't be developed and we wouldn't have opportunities to place anything into action what we have learned. Speaking of opportunities, let's make sure our mirror is clean so we can use it for this next paragraph. All squeaky clean? Alrighty then, check out that shine and clear image! Just don't get too close… Oops, too late!

Welcome to the Mirror World...

I'm sure some might be able to read this without even using a mirror.

It wouldn't be hard.

You would basically just have to read the words backwards from right to left.

I wanted to have this in my book for two reasons really...

One was for the simple fact that I just wanted to mess with people.

I want to get them to think.

To actually have them grab a mirror and do something different.

The other was to really put a spin on perspectives.

At times we don't see things clearly.

Be encouraged to think about change.

Regardless of the situation or circumstance.

We need to choose and look at them from a different point of view.

Sometimes we live our lives totally backwards.

If you're reading this by using a mirror you're living backwards now.

Well... only to a point. I'm sure you get the point.

Find ways to improve or even make things easier.

Yet, easier is not always the easy way out...

In this case, by taking the mirror away, this would confuse some people.

I'm sure some are already confused so let's go back to the real world.

Now which mirror was it... Hopefully this one...

Wow, ok... now where were we? Have you ever thought that before? Years go by and later down the road you finally come to a conclusion in relation to, "How did I ever get stuck in this mess?" We sometimes get used to the disorder so much; it just becomes our regular order... It's what's on the menu without even thinking about it as it becomes a regular routine. It's like ordering a six pack and a pound, then years later finally waking up realizing this isn't food. Wake up. Fight for your life. Make a choice to go after what's most important and own it! Take it! Give it all you got and if you get knocked down, get up going after more. Choose to never stay in a state of emptiness, waiting for life to come as you want it. We can't rely on life to just give us what we think we deserve. The world still moves with the people in it regardless if you're not. We must choose to move, or we'll get moved. *Bing* Right into a locker.

Remember any bullies out there? Possibly slamming others into lockers? Well, I've come to realize that deep down inside, they are hurting as well. Possibly even hurting worse than the people they choose to pick on. Regardless of who you are in this world, we all need some type of love. A love that never dies. A love that lifts you up and accepts you for who you are at this very moment. I thank God for His Love. It's the Only Love that can do just that. Speaking of lockers, remember that *strange key* that we found? I believe it had "U812" imprinted on the side. This locker just so happens to be U812... strange. I believe all things happen for a reason. Why don't we unlock this and see what's on the other side? As we open up the bent out of shape locker, we notice that the only thing inside is a piece of paper. What!? Just Great! I can imagine a lot of people wondering, "You got to be kidding me!" A piece of paper huh... Well, I know where you can cram that! Calm down... it will be ok. Yup, to most it might just be a piece of paper...

A lot of times we go through so many trials and tests, yet the rewards are so small. We at times miss the whole picture. We miss the fine print in the writing and choose not to read between the lines. All the hardships and trials we face truly happen for a reason. Be encouraged to grasp a hold of all you gain out from them. Be encouraged to look at them from a different point of view. Cling onto the experience and knowledge gained. Use the understanding gained for the better to enhance your purpose in life. Change your perspective and see what type of positive picture comes out from it. Let's take a look at that "piece of paper" again, shall we? We could have chosen not to scan the piece of paper, crumbling it up and throwing it away. However, you then wouldn't have discovered *a hidden code: 04-13-07*. I'm assuming these numbers are most likely a code that cracks a safe. If you want to find out what's in the safe you'll have to read on to Chapter 09. Are you willing? If so, you'll have to at least make some type of effort to turn the page.

Chapter 09

Disappearing World

The world, as you know it... Is it alive – full of energy and color? Is it dead – full of death, darkness and despair? I suppose this might depend on where you live or how you are living your life. This might even include how others are living their lives around you, however the way others live should not affect your focus towards your destination. The destination is not as important as the way we live to get to our destination. We should still be able to accomplish the plans and goals in life that you have in mind. We are responsible for the outcome of our own lives. At times we put or place the blame on others, yet we chose the choices which place ourselves in the position of where we are at today. Many of us become sidetracked throughout the day and lose focus. I believe it helps to accomplish one thing at a time, starting with whatever is most important. Now, when you think of most important – Is it more important to you or is it more important for others? When we learn to work as a team, we choose to do what is more important for others to help better the unit. If it's only for ourselves, then we as individuals become stronger as others possibly become weak.

Sometimes we choose to adapt to our surroundings. Depending on where you are at, this could be either good or bad. Would you want to adapt to an area that has been vandalized, eventually becoming part of the problem? Deep down I'm sure we wouldn't, yet at times people are sucked into this life style. It's time we stood up and become part of the solution. We need to love on others showing them a way out. Believe me, there is no true peace, joy or happiness living in an environment that has a negative impact and binds people in. If we are living close by an area that needs help, choose to stand out and complete what is more important. Have a neighborhood clean up, producing a clean sweep around the blocks. Help our neighbors anyway we can by restoring our community. You might ask why? "Why should I?" "It's not like I placed all this junk in the street or on the sidewalk." You might not have, yet aren't you tired of seeing it daily from year to year? Many of us choose not to do a thing because we believe there is no reward. I'd like to correct that statement by placing a positive spin on it. We need to think of the positive and not the negative all the time.

It seems at times we are so blinded by our own selfish ways and desires. We choose only to lift ourselves up when others are dying out there. Some might be just a few feet away from you right now. Has our nation lost hope? Have we as people, lost heart to place others before ourselves? I can type you this, blessing others truly is joyful. When we choose to step out from our own fleshly desires to see others succeed, I believe we are rewarded. There's a reward alright. You might not be able to spend it or drive it, but I guarantee you'll be able to feel it. It's just up to us to not only read these statements of truth, but actually place them into action. Some reading this might have the mind set of, "Yes... I'll feel it alright." "I'll feel it in my neck and my back as I try to get out of bed in the morning."

This could be true; however I'm not talking about that type of feeling. It's more along the line of seeing a cleaner side and view. Why is it more along the line all the time anyway? Let's change it up a bit. It's more along the triangle of feeling a spark in your heart, knowing you're making a difference. It's more along the circle of not being a complete square. The more I'm on this same line, I realize it can bend and form into different shapes... different views and positive results! It's more along the underscore to place what is most important into action. I challenge you to be a part of the solution and believe you can make a change. Regardless of how much money we have or even how much we may think we lack, there is always something we can do. Sometimes all people need is a little breakthrough or momentum to get going. Maybe, just maybe you might be the inspirational speaker that pierces the streets. Literally splitting the concrete with your voice as you get others attention. Speaking of breakthroughs, have you ever just wanted to break away from it all? Yes, I'm talking about breaking the concrete walls we place up in our own lives, in our own minds. We choose not to talk about issues or even willing to produce some type of change. Most of us want to get away from it all before it all just comes back and eventually breaks us. Regardless of who we are in the world, we all face some type of issues in life.

At one point in my life I didn't like the world I was living in, so I decided to create my own. Instead of standing out, I chose to dig myself into a place of isolation. I separated myself from this world and created my own. A world where I could escape to. Escape from what you might ask? Escape from the pain, the conflicts and abuse. Escape from the rules and regulations that were set around me. Escape into a world that only existed inside me just to feel free. At one point in time, the world that existed inside myself, felt more real than this reality. This world was inside my mind. Hope you don't mind, yet I'd like to type a little bit about what's on my mind in regards to my mind. Do you mind? Like I haven't already spoke my mind anyway? Overtime I didn't know which way was up or down, yet alone left or right. I can assure you that even though this felt like freedom, I realize now it truly wasn't. It was more like a prison binding myself in just to feel comfortable. I didn't realize the danger of isolation until it was too late. Isolation actually cuts us off from interacting with others, in which if I was still in that state of mind, the book would have ended a long time ago and would have never got accomplished. Breaking free from that allowed me to express how I truly feel. I'm sure most would not appreciate a book that was sealed shut. After purchasing it, either you can't open it or even once it is finally open only a few words are in it. It could be quite painful I suppose.

To help with issues like pain, loneliness or fear, I chose to stay in a state of isolation, separated from the real world. Growing up, I placed myself in my room playing video games. I loved the feeling of actually having the control of someone else. I loved beating a video game and achieving high scores or trophies. This made me feel like I've accomplished something even though in all reality, I was just sitting in front of a television with a controller for hours on end. Later, I got really heavy into movies. I loved watching all the latest action films and comedies. I have to say, eventually it felt like I was a part of the movie or game and it felt like I was becoming someone. Eventually that seemed to get old, so I moved on to something else. I used and abused many substances, yet I also chose to abuse my gift of art. I've always loved art, so I started using my artistic talents as a form of solitude. Anytime I was upset, mad or angry I would place myself inside my room and draw. I would literally draw for hours upon hours, only drawing images that were in my head. I believed that I could use this gift and talent to produce something that has never been thought of.

I loved abstract art. Art that appears to be non realistic, but seeks to achieve its effect by combining different forms. An art in which was to me, out of this world. Art, which in its sense, is designed so that others can come up with different reasons or meanings to what the painting or drawing is to them. There was no end to the possibilities. I now know that all of my old "Dark Syde" art was all part of a non realistic world that I created. If I wasn't drawing abstract, then the only realistic thing for me to draw at that time was drug related material. My mind was even focused on a sad state of considering women as if they were some piece of meat. Women are not something to be picked out from a line at a buffet. They are truly someone's daughter and even more so, God's creation. The world we live in has placed so much of a negative spin on that subject; it's poisoning our youth. We believe sex is ok before marriage and go along with the simple statements of reasoning things. "Everyone is doing it, It's ok." We find fake fulfillment in giving into these beliefs and when someone isn't good enough anymore, we dump them to the side of the road and find another. Even though we don't see it at the time, these forms of isolation only drag us further away from people and deeper into our own pain. It only gets worse if we choose to continue down that path.

Eventually I set myself aside almost completely from the world. All I wanted to do is live inside my car. It was something about the fact of consistently moving. I had no plan or destination; I just drove and felt free. As time went on, I lost sight of reality. Even though I lost sight, I had a clear focus on what I wanted. I wanted true peace. I wanted true freedom and joy. I was bound up in so much, hoping that there was freedom and peace, yet all that was found was complete emptiness. The happiness that was felt only lasted for a period of time and I wanted more. Truth is we can't find happiness in things. We can't find happiness in our desires. Truth is, this type of so called Joy or Happiness is completely fake. It only robs us from becoming who we truly are designed to be. Truth is, eventually I wanted a way out from the world even I created. I knew I couldn't just drive right out from my mind, because then I wouldn't exist. I know, why don't we drive to an ATM, because money solves everything. Hope you don't believe in that lie. Wait, this is a funny looking ATM – no card slot, just some dials to spin.

Even in our own lives some have wondered what it would be like to spin the dial. Either getting a large sum of cash or possibly wining a trip to an exciting getaway. Again, this type of happiness only last a short while. Instead of rambling on, why don't we try to crack the safe? Remember that code that was found on that piece of crumbled up paper? _a hidden code: 04-13-07_. Let's try that! Now was it right to left or left to right? Regardless we must have the confident knowing we will eventually get it right. We all make wrong choices and mistakes, but the ones that succeed are not afraid to make an executive decision. And even if that goes wrong, at least live to learn from it. "CRACK!" I'm not talking about the drug either! I'm talking about the safe. Inside the safe we find _a Bible_! Some might ask, "Now why would a Bible be in a safe?" Yes, even though it was found in a safe, the safe was in my mind. I'm talking more along the line of what we keep "safe" in our own minds, in our own hearts. What is it that we choose to protect the most in life? Family, friends, possessions... Where is our "safe" place? What in life do you turn to the most? I can assure you the Bible is LIVING and ALIVE. Some find that a Bible is not a way out from what we face. I'd like to talk about this in the next chapter on how much the Bible means to me now and what I've gotten out from it. I wanted an exit, it does exist, yet I didn't know where to start. Ok, so let me start here... wait, that would be the finish, because this is the end of the paragraph.

Ok, back to the start. Jesus is the ONLY one that could set me free from this reality. Even though I built it and created it within my mind, it's like I lost the key to my escape. I was so bound and far into this world that I just knew – HE was my only escape! But we can't just come to Him as an escape, we need to develop a relationship with God. "WHAT!?" Yes, you can actually have a relationship with God. "Crazy?" No, I'm just being real. "Lyin?" No, I'm human. Our minds are consistently at war, in which we choose to let it ramble on and on and on and on. I could just keep on typing "on and on" and make no since, but let me change those two words to "make sense". We have the choice to choose. We ourselves have the same choice in turning off our minds. We control our minds, not our minds control us. If we just pull our heads out from our behinds and actually clean the crap out from our ears, we just might have the ability and confidence needed to tell our minds to be quiet. To be clean! All followers of Christ should be able to hear from Him regardless of the circumstance or situations we face. Believe and have faith. It can be a bit painful breaking free and producing change, yet I've come to realize that it's painful because we are dying to our own flesh. We need to choose to do things that are on a positive basis, which we normally would not do.

Being inside a reality that wasn't real was hard to break free from when I placed myself there for years. Entering back into the real world took quite some time. Time to relearn. "Relearn what?" You might ask. Well, practically discover how to live life all over to a certain extent. I had to relearn how to drive and to change the way how I communicated with others. I was so trapped that my body was used to doing many things while under the influence. It's like I couldn't function properly unless I had some type of substance to make me feel normal. My body didn't know how to respond or react while being sober. In a way, I lost the art of communication, thinking others wouldn't understand or believe, I believed there was no hope.

I can assure you, THERE IS HOPE! It does take time to place new and improved things into action. Ok, so yes it does take time. Simple fact is, are we willing to do it? I mean, "WHY NOT!?" What's the harm in trying something new when we know that years upon years have been wasted? The worst case scenario is that you'll just waist a few more years placing advice into action. Yet "waste" will not be an issue because change and development will take place. We must choose to believe and speak positive! It truly is amazing knowing the old life is wasting away! We need to communicate with one another, being real and open about what we are going through because most of the time people can't read minds. Obviously you know your reading mine as I type, but I have no idea what you're thinking at this moment, unless it's the words that you just read. If we choose not to communicate and talk about our problems or situations in a gentle manner, then no opportunity for help will be available. We should be here to help one another, striving to see others succeed far beyond ourselves.

Some are shy or don't want to talk about what they have been through, possibly having a fear of being laughed at. Some think that others just won't understand. Some might even have a fear of being labeled for the rest of their lives in the town they are in. We think of the most possible worst case scenarios and play them out in our minds before they might happen. I say might, because we don't know what the future holds. We will never know until we choose not to have fear get the best of us, but rather live in peace. Seek the help and advice from those willing to lend a helping hand. Not only seek it, but actually follow through by placing it into action. Knowledge and Wisdom is NOTHING until it's actually ALIVE!

By alive, I mean actually living it out. We must choose to take a stand going upon a path to absolute freedom! Not only just "stand" but to "stay" on the path. It's so easily to get entangled and lured back. The world surrounds us with pressure and advertisements, making us believe that we are not good enough. We believe in order to be good enough or be accepted we must follow through with what the world says to do. Be encouraged to develop your stance of self discipline. If we are in need of saving money, then why do we choose to buy that coffee every day? I mean do the beans literally cry out, "Drink Me!" Or is the aroma so strong that our senses go crazy leaving us senseless or should say cent less? Ok, maybe it's not coffee... yet something is in the way, blocking us to save if we can't. Again, we must choose. This possibly could just be the reality of being happy with what we already have. And if we feel that we might have too much, then why not sell some things? Sell so much stuff that the dog thinks it's next! "ARrr?" Ok, maybe saving money is not a problem in your personal life... But what is if anything at all? I have come to the conclusion of sacrifice.

We must choose to sacrifice time or other things our flesh wants to do in order to produce life of what is really more important. At times this can be painful, but I can assure you it's truly worth every second suffering. If I didn't choose to sacrifice time and other things, this book would have never been produced. If I chose not to discipline myself getting this done and making it a priority, then this page would be blank. Mmmm, maybe I should throw in a few blank pages to throw some of us off? Like I haven't already. Out of all the things that were accomplished through me during sacrifice moments, I've seen others lifted up, grasping a hold of a little more hope and encouragement. I've seen eyes shine and sparkle, stating that they CAN do this. I've seen expressions light up that say, YES – I truly am somebody and am worth something. I've seen others blessed through the discipline and sacrifice being laid out. There are many that are less fortunate in the world, yet as our world disappears, their world becomes opened wider, full of a bright beginnings and even brighter outcomes.

Chapter 08

Eye Ate

How precious our eyes are. What we choose to focus and dwell on really does have an impact on us. As these words are read, it's like our eyes are eating up every word. We soak up all the words we read, impressing the knowledge and eventually having an opportunity to express what we've learned. At first I was going to write only one sentence for this chapter and I was going to entitle it I ate. Then it hit me like a ton of bricks. I was open to so much more. I realized I would have been feeding my flesh and not producing what the spirit wanted. Overtime we all get hungry. Our body becomes weary and needs food to survive. I could type about eating burgers and fries, filling our appetite up with junk. Even reading about food can make others hungry. Then the sunset on me. Why is the saying usually, "It dawned on me" anyway? I suppose because we are waking up to something new, but what about going to sleep with something new too? I mean, if we wake up to something new without learning something new from the other day... Then did it develop in our dreams? I'm sure this could happen, however It'd be nice to learn something new to place into action for the next day. So, what are we filling ourselves up with? I know most of the time it's food, in which that's why I originally was going to call this chapter I ate. Let's face it, we stuff our faces all the time with junk that tastes so good. We get full and our satisfied. Yet only our stomachs are full. What about our spirit? Days go by and most don't feed our spirit, simple fact is we tend to starve it.

You just might be wondering why I entitled this chapter "Eye" Ate. Well, you see, your eyes are literally eating these words up, filling your heart and soul up with knowledge and information. What we choose to feed on, is and will be what we hunger. If we develop a pattern of consistently living a destructive lifestyle, then we will grow up wanting to do more – not only to ourselves, but others as well. If we choose to feed ourselves up with fast food all the time, our bodies will crave that. We won't become satisfied until we indulge in what we crave for. This not only goes for what we eat and do, but also includes what we even say or see. When we speak negative all the time, this will just develop further into more hatred and profanity. I've noticed even when I tried to quit talking in a negative manner, it's not that easy to just quit. It takes time, effort, and self control.

What we choose to read and watch really does impact us deeply too. If we tend to focus our attention on junk full of hatred, lies, and destruction... Well, then we are obviously filling up our hearts and our soul with the same thing. If our hearts are full of destruction and vulgar language, then it will show in our actions. In other words, what we tend to intake and sow into our own lives, we will reap the same exact thing. This not only impacts us, but it also tends to influence others around us. I mentioned in the last chapter that I would talk about the Bible and how much it means to me. I'm going to do just that. It's a lot more than just "reading" the Bible too. These are more than just plain black and white words to make sentences that make sense. To make further sense, they are living words of life! When read and digested properly, then we are illuminated. We must choose to apply the knowledge and information we receive in and through our own actions. Literally taking to heart what is asked of us to do. I know all of our souls long for living truth, yet we must place God first.

Matthew 6:33 states, "But seek first his kingdom and his righteousness, and all these things will be given to you as well."

At times, many of us place other things before God. We choose to place our items, our own priorities, our family and friends before God. I have learned to make God and His calling for my life a priority over anything else. I must choose to place Him first, because the more I seek Him and allow Him to move in my life, the more He is able to pour out - moving into all other areas of my life. Many of us try to find peace, joy, happiness in stuff or family or even friends. We go from one person to the next, from one item to the next. We want more and never seem to get full. We are never satisfied. Coming before the Lord, I actually do get full. I get full enough to pour out into others lives as His Spirit overflows inside me. I'm so enthused at times, consistently being poured out to a point where I'm dry and drained. Now, if I choose to stay in that state of emptiness I'll become miserable. We also have to look at it as an opportunity to continue the process, coming back to God and allowing Him to fill us up by His living words that only He provides.

As you fix your eyes upon this chapter, you'll read a lot of commentary directed by the Spirit that lives in me. *1st Corinthians 6:19-20 states, "Do you not know that your bodies are temples of the Holy Spirit, who is in you, whom you have received from God? You are not your own; you were bought at a price. Therefore honor God with your bodies."*

1st John 4:19-21 states, "We love because he first loved us. Whoever claims to love God yet hates a brother or sister is a liar. For whoever does not love their brother and sister, whom they have seen, cannot love God, whom they have not seen. And he has given us this command: Anyone who loves God must also love their brother and sister."

God loves us so much He was willing to send His son, Jesus, to come down to earth as a living sacrifice for all our sin. In doing so, it's like grace and love exploded from there, sending forth His Spirit. He not only provided a way to Heaven, yet even sent forth His Spirit so that we can finally live. It's about a relationship. I'm sure that a lot of people would take care and treat others with respect when it's someone they love. However, some could care less when it comes down to our own bodies. What we eat, where we go, what we say, what we do. In all reality, what we choose to do with our bodies really does affect the Holy Spirit as well. It's good to stay in shape and exercise, yet building up the body of Christ is done through not only reading His living word, yet also walking it out. The Holy Spirit is a person, in which by honoring Him should be shown in action. We must choose and humbly accept Him. It is a choice. His Spirit is willing and able to live in us as we lay down ourselves, seeking after God and His will – not our own. Since His Spirit is living in us, it's vital on how we choose to live as well. If we truly Love Him, our love should be evident in and through our actions. Let's face it, we can't have a healthy body if we choose to eat nothing but junk food. The same goes with living for God and knowing that His Spirit lives in us. We can't have a healthy relationship, going after God and seeking Him if we consistently feed our fleshly desires. We must choose to put those to death and be willing to place what the Spirit is leading us to do. Also, since we are among a body of believers – they have the Spirit of God in them as well. If we have any hatred towards our brothers or sisters, then it's like we are destroying God's Temple. We must learn to love one another regardless of faults and mistakes.

In other words, we can not and will not be able to Love God if we choose to continue to speak harshly about our brothers. This goes for not only speaking, but even thinking it about them as well. If something about another person drives us to a point of rebellion, then it's something in us. Nobody is forcing us to unleash in a certain way. It's lies we believe about ourselves, it's unforgiveness that is bound up so tightly it only hurts ourselves. We can't expect to live perfectly since no one is perfect, yet the beauty of it all is that God sees us as perfect in and through His sight. Love is, for us, a constant action to grown in. We can never achieve the highest standard of Love, because if that were possible – then we, ourselves, would be God. Only God supplies us with His truth, mercy, and knowledge to express Love toward others. We can't force it, having it come from only us because all in all, God deserves the Glory. We Love, because God Loved us first.

Ephesians 4:29-32 states, "Do not let any unwholesome talk come out of your mouths, but only what is helpful for building others up according to their needs, that it may benefit those who listen. And do not grieve the Holy Spirit of God, with whom you were sealed for the day of redemption. Get rid of all bitterness, rage and anger, brawling and slander, along with every form of malice. Be kind and compassionate to one another, forgiving each other, just as in Christ God forgave you.

Be encouraged to build others up, helping them become successful in life. Help them and lead them on the right path out of love and respect. God longs to be with us and hear from us. However, when we do sin, The Spirit has no choice but to go away. The Spirit wants no part of any sin that we commit, but does still love us. I'm sure you've heard the expression, "Love the Sinner, Hate the Sin." Well, I do believe The Spirit is saddened by the fact when sin occurs. However, since He still Loves us, I also believe that The Spirit is more saddened that He has to leave, knowing he longs for us. He wants to be a part of our lives and have a deep relationship with us. This can not occur if we choose to continue to be lead astray, stiff arming The Spirit of God as He is trying to talk to us, leading us in the right direction and guiding us to the proper destination. The Spirit wants to be seen in and through our actions by expressing Himself how He wants. We must learn to yield to His calling by stepping outside of our comfort zones allowing Him to be in control.

1 Timothy 2:1-4 states, "I urge, then, first of all, that petitions, prayers, intercession and thanksgiving be made for all people— for kings and all those in authority, that we may live peaceful and quiet lives in all godliness and holiness. This is good, and pleases God our Savior, who wants all people to be saved and to come to a knowledge of the truth.

God doesn't want anyone to go to Hell. He is a loving, kind, compassionate God. He truly does long to hear from us, having a relationship with us. Bottom line is that we actually choose to go to Hell by fulfilling our own fleshly desires and stiff arming the word of God, thinking our way is better and that we don't need help. Our appetite for God must mature to become stronger and firmly planted deeper into His foundation. Our souls long for Him. I know a lot of people would rather be lazy and soft, however that is not how we become a spiritual champion. We can't just sit back and relax, expecting God to do all the work. We must choose to take a step towards him. A leap of faith is not writing a couple sentences to this book and saying it's done... I guess writing isn't my thing. No, it takes time and patience. We must learn to not only allow God to be a part of what we do throughout the day, but more so be willing to do what He wants us to do every day, which is so much more successful and satisfying.

1st Corinthians 10:13 states, "No temptation has overtaken you except what is common to mankind. And God is faithful; he will not let you be tempted beyond what you can bear. But when you are tempted, he will also provide a way out so that you can endure it."

I believe God allows things to happen in our lives all time. The trials and situations we go through will either make us or break us. I know that God will help us learn from these situations, giving us knowledge and understanding from them. Simple fact is, are we relying on our own strength to pull through OR are we relying on God as we cry out to Him – having faith, that someway – somehow HE will help us. When we rely on our own strength we don't nearly become as successful or gain any experience out from situations. Most of the time, we break to a point of seeking some type of other way to cope with the issue and turn from the problem, rather than facing it. Only God can give us the strength and understanding we need to succeed and endure anything that we walk through. When we rely on him, He is faithful and will help us pull through. At times, it may not be as "WE" expect it to be or want it to be... Yet, God is faithful if we are willing to have patience while we continue to pursue and seek Him.

I believe at times we break, because we are not relying on God. We believe our own way is better and want to walk out situations without any help. This can be a pride issue, yet if we are not willing to humble or surrender ourselves we will never gain or receive the fullness of the transformation taking place. True growth and change comes from relying on God and submitting our flesh to His way. Even if we force ourselves to do what God is calling us to do, we will not gain full understanding or experience from it. As we are forcing ourselves to do something, most of the time we will have a negative attitude about whatever it is we are doing. Hardly any change or transformation takes place since we are not at peace. Our minds are more focused on the problem than the solution. God does not tempt us, yet He does test us. We pretty much are tempted by our own desires, which don't line up with God's Will.

James 1:12-15 states, "Blessed is the one who perseveres under trial because, having stood the test, that person will receive the crown of life that the Lord has promised to those who love him. When tempted, no one should say, "God is tempting me." For God cannot be tempted by evil, nor does he tempt anyone; but each person is tempted when they are dragged away by their own evil desire and enticed. Then, after desire has conceived, it gives birth to sin; and sin, when it is full-grown, gives birth to death.

Matthew 11:28-30 states, "Come to me, all you who are weary and burdened, and I will give you rest. Take my yoke upon you and learn from me, for I am gentle and humble in heart, and you will find rest for your souls. For my yoke is easy and my burden is light."

We must be willing to learn from God. If we are not willing to surrender our lives or the situation over to Him, then we will never learn from Him. God does make our paths smooth. He stands firm on His promises. We must choose to come to God when we have problems or issues we are facing. I know that in my personal life, I've experienced much more peace and joy when I humbly choose to come to God rather than some pills or alcohol. Many choose to turn to other things, other than God. They think these items, people, or substances will help lighten the load – when in all reality we think it provides happiness and takes our problems away. It may provided a little bit of happiness for only a moment, however deep down inside we are still hurting. We are the ones that make the gospel harder than what it really is. In all reality it's simple. I urge you to draw near to God, because I know He will come. We must choose to come to Him first and then act on what He informs us to do. A relationship takes time, yet it's time willing to be spent wisely. The best relationship any of us can have is with God.

Jeremiah 29:11-13 states, "For I know the plans I have for you, "declares the Lord, "plans to prosper you and not to harm you, plans to give you hope and a future. Then you will call on me and come and pray to me, and I will listen to you. You will seek me and find me when you seek me with all your heart."

The Lord truly does have awesome, amazingly beautiful plans for our lives. In order for us to take captive and grasp a hold of His perfect will for our lives, it's up to us to draw near to God. We must choose to humbly seek him, truly laying down and sacrificing our own plans to see His revealed. These truly are not easy words to hear when our focus is elsewhere other than on Him. If it's on our own past, focusing on the dirt we got ourselves in, then our own lives will reflect that. If it's on doubt, then faith is not part of the outcome and we have already given into defeat. God says that we are victorious, more than conquerors because greater is He who lives in me. What we choose to focus on and believe truly does matter. We must learn to control our minds, turning back to God and to truly be willing to go where He calls us and say what He wants to say through us. Even during the tough situations we face, the only way to find contentment is to truly allow God to be in the midst of all our circumstances and situations. Believe and speak positive, for God stands on His promises and His Love never fails!

2nd Corinthians 12:9-10 states, "But he said to me, "My grace is sufficient for you, for my power is made perfect in weakness." Therefore I will boast all the more gladly about my weaknesses, so that Christ's power may rest on me. That is why, for Christ's sake, I delight in weaknesses, in insults, in hardships, in persecutions, in difficulties. For when I am weak, then I am strong.

This verse is clearly stating that we must cry out to God in our times of weakness. In our times of trouble, in our times of hardship we must choose to ask God for His strength and power to pull us through. God supplies us with the ability to succeed so that He will be glorified through it. All in all, it's God that deserves all the glory, not us or others. Many boast about their gifts and talents. Many choose to glorify themselves, not acknowledging God in the process. Many choose to even give the glory to others, when God was the one that made it happen. In my personal life, God has equipped me with His power so that I can overcome situations that would drag me down. I'm able to be more than a conqueror! I'm victorious because greater is He that lives in me. God has amplified my gifts and talents he has already blessed me with, even revealing hidden ones that I never knew I had. As I learned to be humble, doing what God has asked; I truly give God the glory because He provided the strength to help me become successful. He has blessed me back abundantly – even more than what I expected.

Matthew 5:13-16 states, "You are the salt of the earth. But if the salt loses its saltiness, how can it be made salty again? It is no longer good for anything, except to be thrown out and trampled underfoot. "You are the light of the world. A town built on a hill cannot be hidden. Neither do people light a lamp and put it under a bowl. Instead they put it on its stand, and it gives light to everyone in the house. In the same way, let your light shine before others, that they may see your good deeds and glorify your Father in heaven."

1st Peter 2:12 states, "Live such good lives among the pagans that, though they accuse you of doing wrong, they may see your good deeds and glorify God on the day he visits us."

It's best to work diligently, placing your heart and effort into all areas of work regardless if others see it or not. I believe some work harder to be noticed while others are around, yet once people leave, sometimes we can become lazy and not work as hard. It's not about getting noticed and seeking that self gratification or even being uplifted in compliments from other employees. If they choose to compliment you, awesome, yet let it truly be from them. I know some put on shows and act out things they normally would never do, just so they can be noticed and make them "look" good. It's best to put down the pride we carry at times, working with a pure heart out of humility to not only better the company, but to see others become more successful than ourselves as well.

I believe anyone that claims they are walking with our Living God, should stand out among the world. His Love should be evident. We must learn to become preservatives. We are called to help stabilize our brothers. As we are open to God, so that He can work in and through us, the atmosphere where his presence dwells will always change for His Glory. Strive for fresh and new awakenings and revelations that God has for us to shine while it penetrates the darkness. As His light shines in and through us, others should see something obviously different. As we learn to be open and allow God to use us so that others will succeed, their eyes will begin to open and praise our Father. For we shouldn't seek the approval of others or even expect others to praise or glorify us. For as we are open vessels being used and poured out, God actually uplifts and exalts us as others praise and exalt Him.

James 4:8-10 states, "Come near to God and he will come near to you. Wash your hands, you sinners, and purify your hearts, you double-minded. Grieve, mourn, and wail. Change your laughter to mourning and your joy to gloom. Humble yourselves before the Lord, and he will lift you up.

I'd like to encourage all the readers that it's up to ourselves on how committed and devoted we want to be. It's up to us how deep we want to have a relationship with God. It's up to us to take that first step, humbly submitting and admitting that we are in desperate need of a Savior. As we learn to cast any pride aside and truly be open, only then God comes more intimate and real in our lives. We must learn and choose to be obedient, following His Living Word and not just listening to it. As we dig into the scriptures, these words are life, which should illuminate us. As our eyes feed on every word written our hearts should be penetrated. There must be some decision taking place where we choose to believe and actually make a stand, placing our trust and faith in God. Not taking scriptures to pick and choose what is more convenient, twisting and diluting the truth, but to truly intake every word and passage, knowing we need change and growth in areas that only God can provide. So, He's calling! Everyone is invited! Who is willing to take that stand!? I want to hear the readers out their say, "I am." More importantly – God wants to hear from you. Cry out, repent of our sins, ask for forgiveness and declare Jesus as Lord and Savior of your life. Ask Him to come to live in us and to change our lives. Jesus is King!

John 15:9-17 states, "As the Father has loved me, so have I loved you. Now remain in my love. If you keep my commands, you will remain in my love, just as I have kept my Father's commands and remain in his love. I have told you this so that my joy may be in you and that your joy may be complete. My command is this: Love each other as I have loved you. Greater love has no one than this: to lay down one's life for one's friends. You are my friends if you do what I command. I no longer call you servants, because a servant does not know his master's business. Instead, I have called you friends, for everything that I learned from my Father I have made known to you. You did not choose me, but I chose you and appointed you so that you might go and bear fruit—fruit that will last—and so that whatever you ask in my name the Father will give you. This is my command: Love each other.

Love is uncomfortable, in which we should be doing something to help others prosper or become successful. I don't believe Jesus was comfortable when He died on the cross for us, however He did follow through with the Fathers will for His life. Jesus knew that this was the only way that redemption would be provided. Jesus knew that by Love relationships will be restored, healing will come, the path will be open and a way will be provided. Love is doing things for others, as we step outside of our comfort zone. I believe most would rather invite others to be a part of what we do INSTEAD of asking them what they want to do. Not only asking, but then choose to follow through with it - showing and expressing Love. Jesus didn't want to follow through with God's will at first. He struggled - Yet knew, "Not my will, but yours be done." Jesus even struggled to a point of sweating blood.

James 1:22-25 states, "Do not merely listen to the word, and so deceive yourselves. Do what it says. Anyone who listens to the word but does not do what it says is like someone who looks at his face in a mirror and, after looking at himself, goes away and immediately forgets what he looks like. But whoever looks intently into the perfect law that gives freedom, and continues in it—not forgetting what they have heard, but doing it—they will be blessed in what they do.

1st Corinthians 13:11-12 states, "When I was a child, I talked like a child, I thought like a child, I reasoned like a child. When I became a man, I put the ways of childhood behind me. For now we see only a reflection as in a mirror; then we shall see face to face. Now I know in part; then I shall know fully, even as I am fully known.

We should be a reflection of who God is. Our actions - expressing kindness, compassion, gentleness, humility - etc... It's time we put away our childish games and behaviors. As we learn to man up to our own mistakes, true growth and maturity is produced. We, ourselves, should be grounded and rooted so deeply into the word of God that as we chase and seek after Him we become a reflection of who God is. When we choose to sin, God's glory lessens only within us and among our lives. He has no choice but to flee since our body is the temple to His Spirit, a dwelling place for His presence - reflecting the Father's Love. The Spirit does not want to be around sin. Only Jesus forgives us by His bloodshed on the cross. We only can become purified by His Love as we choose to sacrifice what is so bound in our lives. As we choose to lay it down at the altar letting go and never picking it back up, this truly opens our hearts up for more of God to come so that his Love will dwell and be expressed. The more that forgiveness is shown, not only in our own lives - but forgiving others as well - THEN, more LOVE will be expressed, in which more of God's Glory will be displayed.

As we learn, choose to stop waiting for someone to love us or someone to do unto us, so we then can do back unto them.... We should be first - as a body of Christ, as believers in Christ. We should be the ones stepping out choosing to Love first, so that God's Love will be displayed. For God Loved us first. That is the ONLY reason why we love today. We should step up, even if we don't "feel" like it. I truly believe that after Love is displayed by following through in action – obeying God's command, even when we don't "feel" like it... Then AFTER the situation, pure Joy comes in to refresh, restore, and renew us. We gain so much more experience, knowledge and understanding. It's essential to have a mindset of giving God Glory in this process as well. Not for others, or for ourselves. This walk is not about "feeling" or sight, but more so by faith.

2nd Timothy 4:1-8 states, "In the presence of God and of Christ Jesus, who will judge the living and the dead, and in view of his appearing and his kingdom, I give you this charge: Preach the word; be prepared in season and out of season; correct, rebuke and encourage – with great patience and careful instruction. For the time will come when people will not put up with sound doctrine. Instead, to suit their own desires, they will gather around them a great number of teachers to say what their itching ears want to hear. They will turn their ears away from the truth and turn aside to myths. But you, keep your head in all situations, endure hardship, do the work of an evangelist, discharge all the duties of your ministry. For I am already being poured out like a drink offering, and the time for my departure is near. I have fought the good fight, I have finished the race, I have kept the faith. Now there is in store for me the crown of righteousness, which the Lord, the righteous Judge, will award to me on that day – and not only to me, but also to all who have longed for his appearing.

We should always be prepared to deliver the Gospel and help save the Lost. We should be open at all times, willingly submitting humbly to what God is asking at this point in time or this day. His Spirit always leads us to Him in a loving manner. His Spirit always directs us to say the right words in a loving manner... IF NOT, then it's not from God and from our flesh out of force to get people to change or listen to the Gospel. One reason why anyone might seem "down" while delivering a message is because they might not be "living" out the scriptures. They might even feel convicted during the sermon. Any message being delivered is more presentable with enthusiasm. The speaker should be excited to be a part of reaching out to others. Sermons are more effective when delivered with power, with truth, and with compassion. People who choose not to live according to the word of God, will go after their own desires or in other words according to this scripture passage – They will believe what THEY want to hear instead of what GOD is telling them, in which the TRUTH pierces the flesh. Our hearts are the wellspring of LIFE. What we choose to focus on really does matter because it enters the heart, which enters the soul – If we are full of light then light will be produced. Others will know we are different and not "of" this world. Yet we are willing to lay down our own lives to help others, to encourage seeing them succeed far beyond ourselves. God's word is living and powerful and should be written on our hearts because if it truly is, our lives will be different and shown in our actions. We, at times, don't even need to "say" we are Christians because others will just know by our actions.

Keeping our head up in all situations and enduring the hardships is truly humbling ourselves to the point of knowing we can't do this by ourselves and desperately need God's help. When we lose focus on God we tend to solve our problems by any other means necessary, finding our identity in items, people, possessions... We do it our way, instead of God's. When we truly endure hardships WITH God's help, he empowers us and exalts us because we are humble enough to cry out to HIM. We are humble enough to lay ourselves down and rely on His strength. When we are weak, He makes us strong empowering us with his Love, Courage, Strength, Peace, etc... Our eyes are opened knowing we CAN do this because all things are possible WITH God, yet we must believe. We are no longer our "old selves". At times people are afraid to change because then others around them will know and see a positive difference, making them weak in a world's perspective. We choose not to hold others accountable because of the fear of how we "used" to be. They don't want to lose their so called personality with their friends or people they know who they are "tight" with. They are afraid of change or even standing for righteousness, making a commitment, not being so attached to other people. Faith without works is dead, so we can't just sit back and relax expecting God to do all the work either...

There are so many scripture passages to tie all this in. This apostle (Paul) is already drained, poured out like a drink offering because He has submitted and committed himself to so much and obeyed / yield himself as GOD spoke through Him. This gives us more opportunity to repeat the cycle and be filled again, but this only can happen by coming to God. We all will receive a crown of righteousness for those who abide in God's word – choose to stay committed and devoted. All Glory to God! Fighting the Good Fight and Finishing the Race is truly relying on Him because Through Him we all are Victorious and more than conquerors. Jesus has already paid it all, but we must believe. His Spirit is in us to help teach and remind us of not only scripture, but the situations HE pulled us through and the experience gained to succeed when future situations arise.

Isaiah 55:8-11 states, *"For my thoughts are not your thoughts, neither are your ways my ways," declares the* LORD. *"As the heavens are higher than the earth, so are my ways higher than your ways and my thoughts than your thoughts. As the rain and the snow come down from heaven, and do not return to it without watering the earth and making it bud and flourish, so that it yields seed for the sower and bread for the eater, so is my word that goes out from my mouth: It will not return to me empty, but will accomplish what I desire and achieve the purpose for which I sent it.*

I believe that God has something for us every day. At times we expect things to happen a certain way, yet they become answered differently than what we have planned. As we stay open to God's calling by faith, we are willing to go. I've come to realize that we even must choose to sacrifice our own plans by setting them aside so that others will be blessed and God will receive the glory. Those who are open and humble truly have a heart willing to go as God commands. I've learned that when I yield my heart and tongue with accordance to His word, I'm being used as an open vessel being poured out as God moves through me. His perfect will is revealed during this time. Even though I'm being emptied, others are soaking it up, becoming full. The more humble we become to pursue Him, to be used by Him... the more open we are so that God will use us, moving not only in us, yet through us to reach others. In obedience with His word and commands, we bring Him Glory as His love is expressed and as the gospel is sent out. His Spirit always speaks out of Love, for God is Love. When I have become emptied so that others have become filled, this gives us an opportunity to seek God and come back to Him and His Living Word so that we become full again. For only God supplies what we need daily to fill our soul, in which our hearts long for Him.

His word will never return to Him empty. He calls us all. I believe if we choose not to obey his calling, not to step out in faith... then God will find another who is willing to go. The ones that are willing to go not only hear God, yet claim His calling and place it in action. They know that He provides the courage and will give them the strength to carry out the command. The beauty of it all is that God is not angry or even mad at the ones that choose not to go. However, He does become sad. He longs for the relationship we have with Him to be fruitful and evident. Any time we sin, His Spirit has no choice but to flee. He can't be around it. If we choose not to use what God has blessed us with for His Glory to reach others, He will find others – for our God is a jealous God. He will strip us of our gifts or talents, giving and increasing to those who are willing to complete the calling.

There are so many more scriptures that tie in beautifully with the words already quoted. Be encouraged to dig into the scriptures and ask God to illuminate your hearts. Ask Him to fill you up with His truth and help change not only your life, but being used as a vessel to change your surroundings as well. There is no formula to acquire when it comes down to pursuing God, just be encouraged to talk to Him and listen to Him, developing that relationship with Him is what it's about. However, if you choose to continue the mathematical procedure upon reading this book, then you would come to find out and know you would just read this book all over again starting at Chapter 07. Before signing out, I'd like to encourage you all one last time, if you got this book for free please pass this on to impact others – all for God's Glory!

AMEN!

52538974R00076

Made in the USA
Charleston, SC
21 February 2016